ADVANCE PRAISE FOR

Between Complicity and Integrity

"This delightful book, Between Integrity and Complicity, is an environmental educator's manifesto on how to live well in relation to communities of others. The stories call on us to do more acting (with inevitable missteps) and less worrying. The author skillfully untangles the roots of complicity, integrity and suffering to show us the colourfully varied microcosm of ecological and social renewal, perseverance, and possibility. This book honours listening to the world in all its myriad ways—it is a found treasure."
—Leesa Fawcett, PhD, Environmental and Urban Change, Coordinator of Environmental & Sustainability Education, York University

"This book explores the existential journeys of leading environmental educators and scholars through illuminating portraits and vignettes in a thoughtfully nuanced manner. It is a timely and notable contribution to the literature."
—Greg Lowan-Trudeau, PhD, Associate Professor of Education, University of Calgary

Between Complicity and Integrity

Constance Russell and Justin Dillon
General Editors

Vol. 17

Nora Timmerman

Between Complicity and Integrity

Educators' Stories in Tangled Times

PETER LANG
Lausanne • Berlin • Bruxelles • Chennai • New York • Oxford

Library of Congress Cataloging-in-Publication Control Number: 2023024376

Bibliographic information published by the **Deutsche Nationalbibliothek**.
The German National Library lists this publication in the German
National Bibliography; detailed bibliographic data is available
on the Internet at http://dnb.d-nb.de.

Cover design by Ann Morton and Peter Lang Group AG

ISSN 1949-0747 (print)
ISBN 9781636672328 (paperback)
ISBN 9781636672458 (hardback)
ISBN 9781636672465 (ebook)
ISBN 9781636672472 (epub)
DOI 10.3726/b20659

© 2023 Peter Lang Group AG, Lausanne
Published by Peter Lang Publishing Inc., New York, USA
info@peterlang.com - www.peterlang.com

All rights reserved.
All parts of this publication are protected by copyright.
Any utilization outside the strict limits of the copyright law, without the permission of the publisher, is forbidden and liable to prosecution.

This applies in particular to reproductions, translations, microfilming, and storage and processing in electronic retrieval systems.

This publication has been peer reviewed.

To my many teachers

Contents

List of Figures ix
Preface xi
Acknowledgments xiii

Part I Questioning 1

1 Encountering Complicity, Questioning Integrity 3

2 Seeking and Sketching Stories Through Portraiture 15

Part II Storying 33

3 David Greenwood 35

4 Madhu Suri Prakash 63

5 Ray Barnhardt 89

6	Educator Vignettes	117
	Tracy Friedel	118
	Connie Russell	121
	Richard Kahn	123
	Sean Blenkinsop	126
	Heesoon Bai	128
	Laura Piersol	130
	Rebecca Martusewicz	132
	Dilafruz R. Williams	135
	Chet Bowers	137

Part III	Learning	141
7	Lessons on Integrity	143
8	So Much Is Possible	169
	List of Index Terms	177

List of Figures

Figure 3.1.	Victim of Corporation Greed	36
Figure 3.2.	The Mystical Moist Night Air	39
Figure 3.3.	Collected Nests	41
Figure 4.1.	Guests Are God	65
Figure 4.2.	Madhu's Backyard Hostas	68
Figure 4.3.	Arranging the Classroom	71
Figure 5.1.	ANKN Patch	91
Figure 5.2.	Ray's Honors	93
Figure 5.3.	Alaska to Aotearoa	104
Figure 5.4.	Chena With Moon	107

Preface

This research required and received approval from the University of British Columbia Behavioral Research Ethics Board (certificate number H09-03051) and the Northern Arizona University Institutional Review Board for the Human Research Protection Program (project number 892803-2).

Acknowledgments

I dedicated this book to my many teachers, and these acknowledgements offer me space to expand on that dedication. With each passing day I feel more and more gratitude for, and more and more recognition of, the many teachers that shape my life and experience.

Starting most broadly and deeply, I acknowledge the cacophonous, riotous, fecund, rhythmic, and fantastically mysterious critters and ecosystems that are woven into my most basic being. On the day-to-day, I see and appreciate you as the plants I cultivate in the garden, food I savor, fur babes I pet, or glorious landscapes I traverse. But I know you are more than I will ever know, that you are the gut flora that keeps me alive and hungry, the cycle of $O2$ and $CO2$ that we mutually breathe and exhale, the orbiting moon that pushes and pulls our collective rhythms, and everything more. I acknowledge that my entire being is made from your history and presence, and that all learning I have done in this book is grounded always in (y)our being.

In my human circles, I acknowledge my parents and siblings for encouraging me to question, for loving me for who I am, for gifting me with genuine trust, and for showing me how to turn work into craft. I gratefully acknowledge my partner, Nina. Nina, my learning from and with you each day is a gift. Your very presence in my life has always been a teacher, quite literally from day one. For this book, I acknowledge how you teach me not only the words and ideas that helped shape so much of what I wrote in my final chapters, but also the feelings in my body and heart of what integrity means. Thank you. And to my partner in parenting and a person with whom I share such rich history and relationship, I acknowledge Mike for years' worth of support, believing in me, and always "having my back." Mike, I continue to learn what generosity, joy, and freedom mean from you. I am so lucky to have you in my life.

Connie Russell and Justin Dillon, as series editors, gave me endless encouragement and patience through this process. Connie, this book is certainly finished due to your incredibly lovely and joyful guidance; I am hugely grateful to you! My mentors for the original form of this work, my dissertation, are some of the best teachers I know. Sean Blenkinsop, Daniel Vokey, and Claudia Ruitenberg, thank you all for your brilliance, inspiration, and support—I think of you always when I imagine teaching and mentoring with integrity. I also acknowledge Marcia McKenzie for providing me excellent mentorship, opportunities to write, and the trust to envision myself as a scholar in my early days of graduate school. I am deeply grateful to the nine educators who wrote vignettes with vulnerability and authenticity, and the three who bravely and generously opened their homes for me to come and learn with them. This book is made possible through your sharing; thank you. Colleagues, friends, and extended family have shaped me and this work in innumerable ways through writing groups, critical conversation, and emotional support. I acknowledge and give my gratitude to you: Kim Curtis, Jessi Quizar, Ari Burford, Dana Caulkins, Mark Lewis, Tallie Segel, Leah Mundell, Julia Ostertag, Briana Galas, Alex Kwiatkowski, Luis Fernandez, Brian Petersen, Sean Parson, Marie Gladue, Kristen Flugstad, Sandra Lubarsky, Ramsey Affifi, Lex Scully, Laura Piersol, Mike de Daannan Datura, Joshua Russell, Hannah Miller, Joe Henderson, Jody Clements, Timothy Cordivae, Liz Caulkins, Francine Porter, Nathan Porter, Sharon Crews, Blue Swadner, Mathilde Gatinois, Peter Friederici, Diana Stuart, Viki Blackgoat, Heather Martel, Ned del Callejo, Alexandra Samarrón, Jayne Lee, Andrew Rushmere, Erika Mundell, Claudia Díaz, Alvaro Luna, Ofira Roll, Ido Roll, Shannon McCune Dickerson, Josh Caulkins, Mara Pfeffer, Madison Ledgerwood, Danielle Austin, Leah Porter, Frankie Beesley, Kelsey Morales, Nailah Coleman, Liz Do, my dissertation sisters from all those years ago!, and all my students.

Finally, I acknowledge my children, Bridger and Alex. The seed of this whole project started with my desire to be good for you, to help you become good people, and to contribute to making the world good for you. You are my most powerful teachers: your freedom as children, your learning, your questioning, your challenging, your insight, and your beauty are always the brightest stars in my sky.

Part I
Questioning

1

Encountering Complicity, Questioning Integrity

Most of us are shocked and disturbed when we learn how our food, clothing, and shelter are produced and the effects of that production. Industrial agriculture, chemical dumping, sweatshops, stolen land, exploited workers, forest fires, melting glaciers, oil spills, rape and pillage… our day-to-day living is built upon mountains of harm and suffering. When we start digging into these problems, we see how they are rooted in systems that we all participate in, though differentially. *We* is a difficult word here—not everyone is implicated in the same ways; our class, race, gender, sexuality, and ability render us responsible in differentiated ways. Yet, most of us living in industrialized societies are implicated in unjust systems in some way. We are complicit.

I remember deepening my knowledge of the injustices in our world during my own education. I learned about how my life—my successes, my purchases, my classes, my desires—was built on systems of oppression. I'm still learning this. Giant pill after giant pill, swallowing this kind of knowledge is hard.

Encountering my complicity became most acute for me when I was simultaneously working on my PhD and raising my first child. Through study, I found words to explain colonialism, racism, sexism, anthropocentrism, heteronormativity, neoliberalism, and so on, a long list of deeply held beliefs and material relationships that result in a multitude of oppressions. And through my parenting, I found examples of how the skeletons of these social, cultural, political, and economic patterns are shared from generation to generation. I saw myself unwittingly passing on these patterns to my own child. The "bones" were everywhere: how we talked, how we ate, who had authority, what was funny, what was good, what was bad. My best efforts to teach something different from the norm felt mere drops in the large, cultural and political-economic ocean within which we swam. And, more often than not, I reproduced the problematic norms as much as I resisted them.

I see it in my own college students now: their anguish, anger, anxiety. As an educator, I have accompanied many students as they discover the deeply layered and embedded injustices tied to their simple acts of eating a salad, buying a shirt, or living in a home. About halfway through the semester, there is a common response. Some students inevitably throw their hands up in exasperation, repulsed by the many systems of oppression, wanting to pull themselves out of their culpability within them. They start planning for escape: how can I stop contributing to this corrupt society, this corrupt educational system, this climate change chaos, this crumbling democracy, this – fill in the blank?? The problems are too big, the patterns too strong to break. "We just all need to go out and live in the woods!!"

When we encounter our complicity, there are several ready-at-hand stories that we may latch onto to help us make sense of our experience. The most common stories, the dominant ones in capitalist, colonizing societies, tell us to internalize the problems. We blame ourselves and look to our day-to-day actions as the locus of contradiction and complicity.

One of the most familiar stories we may tell ourselves, or have others lay upon us, is the story of the hypocrite: "If you care so much about climate change, why do you have a car?!?" As climate activist Bill McKibben (2013) wrote, "I've heard it ten thousand times myself—how can you complain about climate change and drive a car/have a house/turn on a light/raise a child?" (p. 15). I ask myself these same questions at times. I balk at climate change, and yet I contribute to it. I study and apply anti-white supremacist pedagogy in my classroom, yet I unwittingly benefit from being white in a white supremacist country. I bemoan the horrendous working conditions in innumerable sweatshops, but even my second-hand clothes are dependent upon them. We all know this story of "the hypocrite."

So, if we go this route, and take up the hypocrisy story, the next common move is to seek removal from all forms of complicity, to stop participating in those terrible, unjust systems and histories (Chang, 2016). Like McKibben (2013) says, we may go without a car, use LED lights, take DEI (diversity, equity, and inclusion workshops), and possibly adopt or not have children. There is a strong desire to find our way out of complicity, to be rid of it in our lives, to stop our participation in unjust systems and histories. Seeking innocence as a way out of the complicity, this story says that if we could only buy green, be kind, and make lifestyle changes, all would be solved.

The story of the hypocrite and "lifestyling" our way to freedom from guilt is one of many stories that make sense of our contradiction and complicity by blaming individual people for systemic problems and ignoring the history of what makes our lives what they are. Understanding contradiction, complicity, and hypocrisy as only a personal problem is problematic and distracting. It ignores the systemic roots of our problems and pushes responsibility for injustice solely onto individual life choices. The systemic roots of complicity are deep and complex. We live in a culture dominated by individualism, a sense of the self as independent, free, as of primary concern over and above social and ecological collectives (Bowers, 2001). We live on a land that bears the scars of colonization, of genocide, and of great cultural and ecological theft that continues to this day (Glendinning, 2002; Tuck & Yang, 2012). We live in a society whose knowledge, wealth, and infrastructure were built on the backs of slaves and that still echoes with blatant racism (Boggs, 2012; Shotwell, 2016; West, 2004). We procure the things we need to live within a capitalist, neoliberal economy that required a colonial, racist history and that builds on individualism through stories of freedom, self-as-market, removal of the social good, privatization, and self-responsibility (Brown, 2015; Harvey, 2005; Klein, 2007).

Sensing complicity, we try to make as many changes as we can, but quickly learn that when we act alone, we can never make enough. This is when some might look to escape as the only option: time to go live in a DIY eco-cabin in the woods. But, if our problems are systemic—if they are political, cultural, and economic—then living in that cabin in the woods is not going to help much more than buying those LED lightbulbs. If even the most diligent and "moral" citizens who dig deeply and transform their lives, are deemed hypocrites, then clearly the problem lies not with them, but somewhere else (McKibben, 2013). If hypocrisy were the problem, then we would be able to fix that problem through our individual choices (Chang, 2016; Shotwell, 2016). But our problems are not that simple to fix.

Seeing oneself as a hypocrite, despairing in the injustices of our complicity, and seeking escape from that complicity is what Alexis Shotwell (2016) calls "purity politics." Purity politics assumes that there is a pristine, clean, pure slate that we can get back to, a way of being that will relieve us of our complicity. She clearly articulates this impossibility:

> Living well might feel impossible, and certainly living purely is impossible. The slate has never been clean, and we can't wipe off the surface to start fresh—there's no "fresh" to start. … All there is, while things perpetually fall apart, is the possibility of acting from where we are. … There is no primordial state we might wish to get back to, no Eden we have desecrated, no pretoxic body we might uncover through enough chia seeds and kombucha. There is not a preracial state we could access, erasing histories of slavery, forced labor on railroads, colonialism, genocide, and their concomitant responsibilities and requirements. There is no food we can eat, clothing we can buy, or energy we can use without deepening our ties to complex webs of suffering. So, what happens if we start from there? (2016, pp. 4–5)

Indeed. What do we make of our complicity in the problems of our day? What do we tell the students who desire so strongly to make change and be good people when they have to face their complicity? How can we live lives of integrity when we know our own complicity? How can we find new stories to explain integrity in the face of complicity?

Researching Integrity and Complicity With Educators

This book originated in my struggles with complicity and my desire to find concrete, experiential stories of how people negotiate it in their day-to-day lives. It is based on research that explored understandings and experiences of complicity, integrity, and the relationship between the two. While there are many relevant contexts within which to explore these questions, I chose to study them in an educational context. Educators are fascinating people to talk to about questions of integrity and complicity because we both resist and reproduce problematic norms. On the one hand, educating is a primary venue through which cultures are reproduced. The dominant ideas, structures, and values of a culture are passed on through compulsory schooling, the procuring of degrees, the media, and sites of informal education. If we recognize that our dominant culture has many ecologically and socially problematic norms, then we must also recognize that education inevitably passes on some—if not most—of those problems as people learn. Particularly within postsecondary contexts, educators do not only pass on our oppressive cultural norms, our very work depends upon them. Postsecondary educators impose hierarchical numbers upon the complex and qualitative process of learning through the use of grades; they fly around the world to conferences to discuss climate change and ensure they are granted promotion and job security; the buildings they teach in and supplies they use spill toxins into local waterways, and the levels of bureaucracy at colleges and universities dehumanize students, turning them into data for the latest grant application (Orr, 1999).

On the other hand, education offers the possibility for transformation. Teaching and learning together about the world allows us to (re)define it and act within it anew—not only in the future, but in our ongoing interactions with one another (Hart, McKenzie, Bai & Jickling, 2009). Thus, even as we recognize how educators perpetuate problematic norms, we also offer opportunities to transform those problems by teaching something more just that aims toward greater flourishing.

My research thus explored integrity and complicity through inquiries into educators' lives. In particular, I turned to postsecondary education faculty with strong philosophies of social and ecological justice. Postsecondary education faculty are both theorists and practitioners of education. They are uniquely positioned to engage in a reflective practice that asks questions about how their lives do and do not reflect their knowledge, values, and/or visions. They frequently hold incredibly critical and creative ethical ideals, yet work and live within large-scale, privileged social institutions that are at odds with those ideals. As one of many examples, many postsecondary educators teach about histories of displacement and forced residential schooling, and simultaneously engage in this work within buildings and campuses located upon unceded First Nations land.

Diving into the rich and complex context of postsecondary educators' experiences, my research sought out lessons for how to work through these kinds of complicity in ways that had some semblance of integrity. I wanted to listen to and learn from experienced, respected educators. I wondered, how do educators handle their complicity in perpetuating the very same problems that their work allows them to identify? What does it look like to simultaneously be aware of contradiction or complicity, work to avoid at least some of it, and also take action in spite of it? What do educators who feel strongly compelled to change actually do, how do they live, and why?

Because there are already ample and impressive theories on integrity and complicity, and because I sought out examples of concrete experiences with integrity and complicity, I chose to focus my research on stories. Story expresses complexity and nuance, it is evocative and compelling, it has the remarkable capacity to elicit care and connection. Sharing stories is a way of opening up educative possibilities instead of closing in on certainties (Barone, 2001). Blenkinsop and Judson (2010) write, "When we learn something in story form, our emotions and imaginations are evoked and we come to feel something about what is being learned. ... [Stories] make knowledge meaningful and, when done well, memorable for the listener" (p. 176). Concrete stories from our lives are especially powerful in the context of academic life, where vulnerability, ignorance, and ambiguity are often shunned. I love Pelias' (2005) explanation of how storytelling holds significant power in a postsecondary educational context. He writes that the authentic and vulnerable sharing of stories from is a kind of confessing, exposing, and witnessing whereby that which is...

> ...hidden is made public, what might have stayed buried is put under examination, what might have been kept as personal commitment becomes public testimony. Such efforts often ask readers to respond, not just at the level of ideas but as one person who has become connected to another. (p. 421)

My research thus became a process of seeking and sharing stories. Over the course of several years, I wrote and/or collected the stories that animate this book. There were two main phases of research, each with distinct approaches to gathering stories. The first phase of research happened during my doctoral studies. For my dissertation, I used a research methodology called portraiture to seek out and write "portraits" of three educators. Portraiture learns from and with respected others through the creation of in-depth relationships, and in turn shares those lessons through "portraits:" literary, non-fiction narratives written by researchers (Lawrence-Lightfoot and Hoffmann Davis, 1997). For the portraits, my participants were three experienced education faculty members with incisive critiques of dominant educational institutions and strong reputations for being advocates of socio-ecological justice. I was lucky enough to work with Drs. Ray Barnhardt, David Greenwood, and Madhu Prakash. The portraits that I wrote of them and their understandings and experiences of integrity and complicity are core components of this book.

After I finished my dissertation research and graduated, many people approached me to talk about the research. Although the postsecondary education context of my study was not applicable to everyone, lots of folks felt that the core questions about integrity and complicity were widely applicable. Additionally, my ideas about the research had evolved, and I felt a responsibility to update how I framed my original participants' portraits. Thus, I began a second phase of research several years after the first had ended.

For the second phase of research, I first updated each portrait. I had more conversations with the original research participants and added excerpts from those conversations to the end of their original portraits. I also increased the breadth of the story-seeking to include nine other postsecondary educators. With these nine new educators, I solicited vignettes from them that explored the core themes of integrity and contradiction using stories from their own lives; these vignettes were written by the educators themselves with my editorial input. These nine vignettes are also a core component of this book. This book is thus a collection of evocative and compelling stories—about educators, by educators, and for educators—that help re-story what it means to live between complicity and integrity in our tangled times.

Re-Storying Integrity

Integrity is a concept that comes from the root "integer," meaning "whole." Dictionaries tell us that integrity means "honesty," "goodness," "honor," and "coherence." In common usage, integrity is often taken to mean the absence of contradiction. This usage implies that integrity is the *"opposite"* of being complicit. Common phrases invoked to describe this sense of integrity are "walking the talk" or "practicing what we preach." Well-known teacher–scholar Parker Palmer (1998) has used the term *integrity* in this way. He says that educators seek integrity when they "can no longer live without bringing [their] actions into harmony with [their] inner life" (p. 167) and must decide "what is integral to their selfhood, what fits and what does not" (p. 13).

On the other hand, there are interpretations of the word "integrity" that do not assume that having integrity and being complicit are mutually exclusive. That is, going back to the root of the word, "whole," integrity is a phrase that can invite us to acknowledge our whole complex selves and communities, seeing them for the complicity that they hold, yet still asserting the possibility of striving for goodness within them. Being honest is acknowledging and seeking out our complicities, knowing that no matter how much integrity we have, we are not working ourselves out of that complicity. Being honorable and good have to do with how we are in our relationships—to other people, places, and beings (Moore, 2016). So, it is possible to be our whole selves—which includes the destruction and injustice we are complicit in (re)creating—and to also still be "honest," "honorable," and "good."

Why this word "integrity?" Some scholars suggest that we shift away from being concerned with notions like integrity once we recognize how "integrity" commonly implies that we individually seek a principled, contradiction-free life, and that this kind of pursuit is both 1) politically unstrategic, and 2) existentially impossible to attain. For example, in Shotwell's (2016) book, *Against Purity: Living Ethically in Compromised Times*, she argues that the notion of integrity is often equated with purity and we have to stop aiming for purity because it is an illusory ideal that arises from a privileged erasure of the vast, complex history of layers upon layers of complicities that people have lived with for ages. She writes, "A great deal of harm is done based on a metaphysics of purity; since it is false and because it is harmful, we do better to pursue metaphysics that do not aim to preserve fictions of integrity" (p. 16). I agree with her argument; living "against purity" is an important political position to take.

However, I don't think it is enough to live "against purity" nor to drop the call to live with integrity entirely, even if common definitions of it are impossible and naive. It seems to me that there is an itch that people are trying to scratch in their efforts to live "with purity" or "with integrity." And the most accessible tools to scratch that itch are the dominant norms of individualistic behavior change and/or unending spirals of guilt over one's own "hypocrisy." But, to simply recognize the problematic roots of that go-to scratch and decide to work against it doesn't relieve the itch.

Living and participating in an unjust world full of disregard and disaster, we need to engage with the challenge of doing something different in tangible ways. We need to feel, see, hear, and touch something that helps us know that living well is possible in the here-and-now, and that at least parts of our living are connected to what we believe in. We need the practice of envisioning the world in which we want to live and working to bring that world into existence. That is one of the most important functions of the pull to live life with integrity. And it is this function and desire that I wish to highlight in this book. It does not serve liberation or flourishing to solely seek out personal solace or a sense of working one's way to innocence (Tuck & Yang, 2012), and that certainly is not what I'm suggesting here. But, I do see in the stories that illustrate this book that there is a generativity, an energy that can fuel long-term collective work, that comes from knowing that we can do things, think things, and act in ways that we believe in.

Across all of the stories and experiences I encountered while writing this book, I learned three lessons that help me re-story the meaning and purpose of integrity. I describe these three lessons briefly below, and the final chapter is dedicated to their elaboration. I learned that, if integrity is an answer to complicity, it is only so if: 1) I tend to how scale matters, 2) I learn to stop being one person, and 3) I act anyway.

I learned that scale matters. Ten years ago, starting my dissertation, my initial goal was to seek integrity as an alignment between my actions and my beliefs. It felt like a common, yet complex desire. As I learned more and more about how I and others unconsciously re-created racist, colonial, heteropatriarchial, and anthropocentric norms, I wanted to change that. I wanted my actions to create a different world based on justice, liberation, and flourishing. Yet, as I engaged with the stories in this book, I learned how much scale matters in the work to create a different world and to consider how "integrity" plays a role in that work. I learned to assess the scale of my values and how they align (or not) with the scale of my response-ability (Haraway, 2016). That is, I re-storied my understanding of integrity away from a general alignment between beliefs and actions writ large, to an understanding that insists upon first understanding the scale of those beliefs and actions so that I critically consider what kinds of goals I pair with what types of action, and who is implicated along the way.

I learned to "stop being one person" by thinking and working relationally. Integrity is most commonly used as a descriptor for individuals, but I learned that integrity is reliant upon our communities—we understand and we practice it in relation to others. Thinking and working as if we are not only one person takes integrity out of a conceptual, idealized realm where something such as "purity" is possible, and into the contingent, contextual actualities of our lives. As creatures that are historically situated, members of some communities and not others, inhabitants of and inhabited by varied ecologies, and always in process/becoming, if we want to aim for integrity, we must think and work toward it relationally.

I learned that I must—we must—act anyway. Whether we blunder head-on into our complicities or we steep in them in a slow simmer, we must act anyway, despite those complicities. Acting anyway means avoiding paralysis. It means using our complicities as sites of learning and places to educate ourselves and one another. Acting anyway means choosing to focus on possibilities, taking complicity and contradiction as a given, as background information, that we will always be failing, making mistakes, being complicit in one system of power or another. When we understand integrity as a process of acting anyway, we commit to the work of creating new visions of what is possible while humbly facing the ongoing, unfolding work of undoing what is broken and stitching together what is possible.

This Book's Purpose

Faced with contradiction, this book asks what living with integrity means in the midst of our many, tangled complicities. It shares stories of educators' experiences and understandings of integrity and contradiction. And, it synthesizes the main lessons that I have found most transformative and instructive for myself as an educator. Although this book explores questions of complicity and integrity in the context of postsecondary education, the questions are relevant in countless other contexts. For anyone concerned with feelings of hypocrisy, contradiction, or complicity, and unsure of how to navigate through them with integrity, I hope that you may find inspiring points of reflection in this book. For future teachers worried about whether and how you will be able to live according to your values in your future work, I hope this book gives you insight and possibilities.

More specifically, there are three key purposes to this book, the first of which is to raise questions about our experiences of complicity, even while critically examining those questions themselves. I trouble the common discourse about integrity and complicity that positions individuals as choice-makers, accountable to themselves, "free agents" within a global, neo-capitalist milieu. Yet, I also want to honor the choices that we do have as individuals and the feelings that arise in our own knowledge of ourselves and the world. So, on the one hand, the purpose is to critique the question of how to live with integrity, but on the other, the purpose is to give time and space for the exploration of that question. In this chapter, I shared the dominant ways we story complicity through narratives of contradiction or hypocrisy. I shared why I don't find these stories adequate, and why I wanted to learn more. In the next chapter, I explain in detail how I went about learning more through research. For readers interested in portraiture as a methodology and precisely how the stories were composed, the second chapter provides this information.

A second—and perhaps the most fundamental—purpose of this book is to explore how experienced and exemplary educators act, think, explore, and negotiate integrity and complicity in their personal and professional lives. So, this book shares stories. It shares stories of the people I have had the privilege of researching in the form of portraits, and it shares short vignettes that I curated and edited from nine other exemplary educators. The second section of this book is composed entirely of these stories. All of the educators highlighted in this section have much, much more to say than can fit in this book. What is captured here are only snapshots, or portraits, of their insights. Yet, these stories offer a diversity of perspectives on integrity and complicity. Because there is no one right answer or recipe for how to answer these questions, hearing from multiple voices is important. Whereas some research seeks out one, specific answer to a question, this book is based on research that seeks multiple answers, stories, and possibilities. As Barone (2001) says, "We are inclined, not toward the securing of even a semi-permanent truth, but, in a playful, exploratory spirit, toward uncovering and expressing alternate (sometimes even conflicting) interpretations of the phenomena under scrutiny" (p. 24).

Finally, another core purpose of this book is to re-story integrity as a concept that can provide meaning even in light of, despite, and in conjunction with our complicities. I thus conclude the book with a chapter that shares what I learned about integrity throughout this research. These lessons push back on dominant concepts of integrity that define it as an individual virtue available only to those whose visions and actions are perfectly in alignment. As I indicated above, this book ultimately argues that, for integrity to be an instructive and transformational value, we must learn how scale matters, how to not only be one person, and how to act anyway.

While this book shares the lessons I have learned about integrity, it does not provide a set of answers to questions of how to live with integrity or how to face complicity with integrity. It is not a recipe book with activities and ideas for educators to try. It will not solve the conflicts or complicities. I do not believe that straightforward answers to these questions exist. Feeling unsure and often lost in what I saw as the contradictions in my own life, I began this project wanting to learn about how others in similar situations work through and with their own complicity. I wanted to listen and learn from experienced, respected educators. My goals for listening were not to emulate, but to reflect and grow alongside wise council, to find new words and ideas that would re-shape my original questions into new inquiries through complex understandings. With gratitude, I am able to say that I have done so. It is my sincere hope that reading this book and these stories will allow you to do the same.

References

Barone, T. (2001). Science, art, and the predispositions of educational researchers. *Educational Researcher, 30*(7), 24–28.

Blenkinsop, S., & Judson, G. (2010). Storying environmental education. *Canadian Journal of Environmental Education, 15*, 170–184.

Boggs, G. L. (2012). *The next American revolution: Sustainable activism for the twenty-first century*. University of California Press.

Bowers, C. (2001). *Educating for eco-justice and community.* University of Georgia Press.

Brown, W. (2015). *Undoing the demos: Neoliberalism's stealth revolution.* Zone Books.

Chang, D. (2016). The sticky side of hypocrisy: Environmental activism in an oil-drenched world. *Philosophical Inquiry in Education, 23*(2), 200–202.

Glendinning, C. (2002). *Off the map: An expedition deep into empire and the global economy.* New Society Publishers.

Haraway, D. (2016). *Staying with the trouble: Making kin in the Chthulucene.* Duke University Press.

Hart, P., McKenzie, M., Bai, H., & Jickling, B. (Eds.) (2009). *Fields of green: Restorying culture, environment, and education.* Hampton Press.

Harvey, D. (2005). *A brief history of neoliberalism.* Oxford University Press.

Klein, N. (2007). *The shock doctrine: The rise of disaster capitalism.* Metropolitan Books.

Lawrence-Lightfoot, S., & Hoffmann Davis, J. (1997). *The art and science of portraiture.* Jossey-Bass.

McKibben, B. (2013, March/April). A moral atmosphere: Hypocrisy redefined for the age of warming. *Orion, 32*(2), 15–16.

Moore, K. D. (2016). *Great tide rising: Towards clarity and moral courage in a time of planetary change.* Counterpoint.

Orr, D. (1999). Transformation or irrelevance: The challenge of academic planning for environmental education in the 21st Century. In W. L. Filho (Ed.), *Sustainability and university life* (pp. 219–233). Peter Lang.

Palmer, P. (1998). *The courage to teach: Exploring the inner landscape of a teacher's life.* Jossey-Bass.

Pelias, R. J. (2005). Performative writing as scholarship: An apology, an argument, an anecdote. *Cultural studies ↔ Critical Methodologies, 5,* 415–424.

Shotwell, A. (2016). *Against purity: Living ethically in compromised times.* University of Minnesota Press.

Tuck, E., & Yang, K. W. (2012). Decolonization is not a metaphor. *Decolonization: Indigeneity, Education & Society, 1*(1), 1–40.

West, C. (2004). *Democracy matters: Winning the fight against imperialism.* Penguin Books.

2

Seeking and Sketching Stories Through Portraiture[1]

In day-to-day experience, how do educators understand, negotiate, name, feel, and live between the notions of complicity and integrity? With this question at the core of this book and the research that informed it, I found that the best way for me to explore the question was through story, using a research approach called portraiture. Because there is no "answer" to the question of "how to live with integrity," I wanted to learn about integrity and complicity in ways that were not prescriptive, but instead offered multiple inspiring possibilities. I needed a research approach that provided space for vulnerability, complexity, and ambiguity. Portraiture was the right methodological approach to help me reach these goals.

Portraiture is a form of inquiry that asks researchers to form deep relationships with participants, explore participants' experiences and ideas about particular phenomena, and write those experiences up into literary "portraits" of participants. Sara Lawrence-Lightfoot coined the term "portraiture" in the 1990s. Lawrence-Lightfoot and Hoffmann Davis (1997) explain that, "Portraits are designed to capture the richness, complexity, and dimensionality of human experience in social and cultural context, conveying the perspectives of the people who are negotiating those experiences" (p. 3). While portraits themselves are often of specific people or learning sites, portraitists dive into those particular experiences with the goal of tapping into something that resonates much more generally. In other words, within a specific story about a specific person and place, lie lessons that apply to other people and places. Lawrence-Lightfoot and Hoffmann Davis describe how storytellers and social scientists alike take this same approach:

> Eudora Welty (1983) offers a wonderful insight gained from her experience as a storyteller. She says forcefully: "What discoveries I have made in the process of writing stories, all begin with the particular, never the general." Clifford Geertz (1973) puts it another way when he refers to the paradoxical experience of theory development, the emergence of concepts from the gathering of specific detail. Geertz (1973) says, "Small facts are the grist for the social theory mill" (p. 23). The scientist and the artist are both claiming that *in the particular resides the general.* (p. 14)

Lawrence-Lightfoot and Hoffmann Davis (1997) look specifically to storytellers and ethnographers in this quote because portraiture itself is built upon a combination of the more recognized methods of ethnography and narrative inquiry. Portraiture is ethnographic through its immersive, descriptive (versus experimental) fieldwork, its interest in a wide variety of meaningful aspects of participants' lives (versus only pre-determined foci), and its categorical, thematic forms of analysis (Goetz & LeCompte, 1984). It is similar to narrative inquiry in its emphasis on aesthetic, story-based interpretation and representation (Barone, 2000, 2001; Clandinin, Pushor, & Orr, 2007; Hart 2002; Richardson, 1997).

Lawrence-Lightfoot and Hoffmann Davis (1997) see the combination of ethnography and narrative inquiry as a way to bridge "the realms of science and art, merging the systematic and careful description of good ethnography with the evocative resonance of fine literature" (p. 6). They describe portraiture as an approach that brings together the "two worlds" of art and science, "allowing for both contrast and coexistence, counterpoint and harmony… allowing [us] to see clearly the art in the development of science and the science in the making of art" (p. 3).

This blending is appealing to my own sensibility as a researcher who has always been interested in arts-based forms of research. The ideal of creating a "systematic and careful description" with the "evocative resonance of fine literature" aligned with my goals of creating research that was inspiring for others to read. Yet, alongside this appreciation, I questioned the way in which Lawrence-Lightfoot and Hoffmann Davis (1997) describe art and science as two separate "worlds," erring on the side of not challenging the dominant associations of science with objectivity and art with subjectivity. In my work, I draw upon others to suggest that both art and science are subjective and aesthetic in their own right (Clough, 2002; Eisner, 1997; Richardson, 1997). The differences between art and science are less about inherent qualities, but are more about different aims. As Barone (2001) explains, while science is interested in "reducing uncertainty," art is more interested in "uncovering and expressing alternate (sometimes even conflicting) interpretations of the phenomena under scrutiny" (p. 24). The stories in this book do both: they dive deeply into explorations of complicity and integrity as phenomena, seeking to understand them better, while also opening space for ambiguity and multiple interpretations.

Portraiture is thus an approach to research that foregrounds the importance and educational value of story as a medium through which to both inquire and share ideas (Blenkinsop, et al., 2022). It brings together ethnography and narrative inquiry to do so, blending careful description with evocative storytelling. In this chapter, I explain portraiture and how I used it in more detail. As a relatively unknown research methodology, my hope with this chapter is to give an updated description of the approach and how it works in practice. My work here overlaps with Blenkinsop, et al.'s (2022) newly published edited book on "ecoportraiture" (in which I have a chapter that is adapted from this one). This recent and growing exploration of portraiture tunes into its potential for not only observing and researching, but also fostering and strengthening, relationships between researchers and the more-than-human world. While my work for this book and the writing in this chapter is limited in how much it explores "ecoportraiture," this chapter may be helpful to other researchers interested in portraiture more generally and will also give the context to understand how the stories that comprise the bulk of this book were created.

Seeking a Complex "Goodness" Through Relationship

One of the foundational assumptions of portraiture is that it is a "search for goodness" (Lawrence Lightfoot & Hoffmann Davis, 1997, p. 9). Most of my colleagues raise their eyebrows when they hear this phrase, concerned about its essentializing potential; it requires some explaining. Seeking out "goodness" in portraiture means that the research is used to better understand what "good" means in different contexts. That is, portraiture seeks context-specific and fluid definitions of "goodness;" it is intended to open up a discussion on what "good" means (relative to the research questions) with participants:

> [Portraitists] are concerned with documenting how the subjects or actors in the setting define goodness. The portraitist does not impose her definition of "good" on the inquiry, or assume that there is a singular definition shared by all... Rather the portraitist believes that there are myriad ways in which goodness can be expressed and tries to identify and document the actors' perspectives. (Lawrence-Lightfoot & Hoffmann Davis, 1997, p. 9)

Thus, seeking out goodness does not mean that researchers "idealize... human experience [or] focus only on good things, look only on the bright side, or give a positive spin to every experience" (p. 141). By seeking out goodness, portraiture actually resists universalized, static definitions of what is "good" and turns toward relational, contextual understandings of goodness, making them the very focus of the research itself.

On one hand, my research aligned well with Lawrence-Lightfoot and Hoffmann Davis' (1997) descriptions of a "search for goodness." Like the authors describe, I simultaneously wanted to learn from participants' experiences and understandings, *and* interrogate those understandings with them. I approached participants as leaders, as whole human beings with faults, but as exemplars, mentors, people from whom I had something to learn and with whom I could deeply engage and interrogate ideas.

On the other hand, my research question and purpose pushed me toward a search for goodness that was more complex and ambiguous because I also sought out the—for lack of a better phrase—*lack* of goodness. I wanted to learn how other people experience and explain both "integrity" *and* "complicity" in their day-to-day lives. Thus, my approach to portraiture's "seeking of goodness" saw me searching for vulnerability, paradox, and complicity in the same breath as I sought out honesty, accountability, and commitment.

To "seek goodness" in ways that reveal not only strengths, but weaknesses, not only confidence, but vulnerability, it was essential that I establish trusting relationships with my participants. Portraits are often not anonymous, and the data collection, analysis, and representation process is a long one. It is one thing to explore the moral ambiguity of our experiences as anonymous people in an anonymous setting in a once-off meeting, but when complex aspects of our lives are explored at length and made public, trusting, ethical relationships are paramount (Kim, 2016). Ethics of care and responsibility thus shape the relationship between portraitists and participants, and between portraitists and the final research portraits.

Ethics of care and responsibility are features of many approaches to research (Bailey, 2012; Castagno, 2012; Kim, 2016; Lemley & Mitchell, 2012; Reimer, 2012). A primary way of tending to an ethic of care in research is through building trust within relationships between researchers and participants. Essentially, this is a process of building care between researcher and participant in such a way that researchers are not accountable only to "the data," but are accountable through their care for the participants with whom they work. Ethics of care, particularly politicized ethics of care (Russell & Bell, 1996; Piersol & Timmerman, 2017), also encourage researchers to tend to the connections between what it is that participants care about in their immediate lives, and how that immediate care relates to larger socio-ecological structures. For example, in my analysis, rather than simply listing participants' concerns, I utilized a politicized ethics of care to identify how those local concerns are rooted in systemic injustices.

Whereas many research approaches might call for separation between researcher and participant, identifying objectivity as the primary indicator of validity, portraiture instead leans on an ethic of care to foster interconnection, responsibility, and care. A benefit of nurturing these values is that the resulting relationships open up the possibility for a fuller expression of complexity and ambiguity in the research. Moreover, care-based relationships with participants are also ends in and of themselves. That is, regardless of whether trust within a relationship can grant a researcher more "quality data" (Kim, 2016), I consider the relationships I created and maintained with participants to be one of the primary "achievements" of my research.

When research depends upon a trusting relationship, the shape of that research changes. My use of portraiture called for reciprocity: if I ask you to share something that makes you feel vulnerable, then I need to be willing to share too. While I did not engage in a kind of tit-for-tat, back-and-forth exchange of information with my participants, given that I was seeking to hear about their experiences, we did spend much of our time talking and getting to know each other. As I asked participants about their families, childhoods, work life, experiences, and inner reflections, it felt only fair that they got to ask me about those same things too. All that sharing built substantial, trusting relationships. Now, ten years after I visited my participants for the first time, when we meet up, talk on the phone, or email, we easily laugh together, cry together, and cherish any opportunity to share a meal together. Thus, I found the creation and renewal of trusting relationships with participants to be one of the most powerful and joyous characteristics of portraiture.

The trusting relationships my participants and I built were important for diving into complex, vulnerable topics, but they were also necessary for creating the portraits (Lawrence-Lightfoot & Hoffmann Davis, 1997). Tending to these relationships helps researchers as they engage in the complex work of identifying voice, storylines, and themes. For example, at the end of this chapter, I discuss how the process of analyzing, writing, and revising Madhu's portrait was deepened by the fact that we had a substantial relationship, making the portrait that much more meaningful. Finally, and as I will discuss more in the following section, the practice of nurturing a relationship allows researchers to acknowledge the co-creation of knowledge between participants, researchers, and their (human and natural) communities. That is, through the creation and renewal of relationships between portraitists and participants, researchers are compelled to analyze and represent portraits as forms of shared/co-created knowledge.

Co-Creating Stories With Artistry

Storytelling is foundational to the process and product of portraiture; story is used to both seek out and share knowledge. In general, listening for and telling stories is simply what we do, as human beings: "Whoever you are, wherever you come from, whatever you do in your life, you're always busy telling a story. ... It's a continual thing, this telling stories" (Profeit-LeBlanc, 2002, p. 47). Given this continual storytelling, all research is a form of storytelling, even quantitative research (Clough, 2002). However, portraiture is particularly interested in storied descriptions of experience and phenomena, and it uses a literary, storytelling form to share knowledge. These choices carry assumptions about valuable knowledge and enable particular kinds of knowledge to emerge (Blenkinsop, et al., 2022).

Identifying storytelling as a location for theorizing draws from feminist and narrative research approaches. These approaches assert the value of lived experience as a place from which to generate knowledge (Fawcett, 2000; Gaard, 2009; Gough, 1999; Hallen, 2000; Harvester & Blenkinsop, 2010; Richardson, 2000). That is, these approaches suggest that the stories people tell to make sense of their lives are the foundation for theorizing at larger socio-cultural levels. Storytelling as a way of theorizing enables people to produce knowledge that is clearly tied to context, community, and that is co-constructed. Richardson (2000) describes how feminists in particular moved away from understanding theory as architecture, and toward the idea of theory as story. Grounding their work regularly in the notion that "the personal is political," feminists assert that the practice of telling and sharing stories about their life experiences, particularly when done iteratively in community, is theorizing. Politics—the negotiation of power—plays out in our day to day lives and experiences. Sharing stories about those lives and experiences, exposing them, identifying trends, collectivizing the narrative, is a liberatory theorizing that centers those most affected or marginalized.

Conceiving of storytelling as a kind of theorizing ties back to the point that Lawrence-Lightfoot and Hoffmann Davis (1997) make (explained above) about how portraiture finds the general in the particular. For example, in chapter six, I begin Ray Barnhardt's portrait with a story about how I had laryngitis during my visit to see him. I write about how my laryngitis meant that I sat back and listened to the First Alaskan folks in Ray's community because I literally couldn't talk, and my own position of listening mirrored Ray's political position of listening and facilitating as a white educator and researcher working in a First Alaskan context. From this specific story, there is ample room to theorize (again, moving from the particular to the general) about power and positionality.

In addition to portraiture valuing storytelling as a location for knowledge creation, portraiture's use of story enables a kind of knowledge to emerge that is contextual, co-created, complex, and aesthetic. Researchers that use narrative inquiry readily acknowledge the temporal, place based, and social nature of stories (Clandinin, Pushor, & Orr, 2007; Kim, 2016). Similarly, portraiture recognizes that knowledge cannot be separated from the people, places, and times with which it was created, and thus often does not hide, remove, or generalize the particularities of people and places (Cheney, 1989). In these ways, portraits push back against the tendency to compartmentalize knowledge in their often-blurred lines between the personal and professional, or the public and private. Thus, portraiture's use of story as a way to share knowledge is less reductionistic than some other methodological approaches. Following the thread of a story, researchers weave their way through categories that might otherwise be used to cut up themes into seemingly discrete pieces.

Additionally, because portraiture listens for story, researchers are given the opportunity to consider multiple storytellers. Lawrence-Lightfoot and Hoffmann Davis (1997) explain a distinction between listening *to* a story, a more passive approach where the researcher "waits to absorb the information and does little to give it shape and form" (p. 12), and listening *for* a story where the researcher is "more active, engaged" (p. 12) during interviews, asking questions that share "the language of the narrative that *we* are co-constructing" (p. 121). When researchers listen *for* stories, they do not attempt to blend into the background; instead, they acknowledge their role in shaping the discussion, identifying the story as co-created.

While Lawrence-Lightfoot and Hoffmann Davis (1997) discuss the co-creation of stories as a process by which the portraitist's and participant's voices work together to co-construct a story, my experience is that the variety of voices involved in the co-creation is much larger. The stories we tell have their origins in a complex milieu of voices coming together at a given point in time. For example, the opening story from Ray's portrait that I mentioned above includes the voices of his mentors, past students, a particularly effective virus, myself as a researcher, and a current political narrative of our time. The story is co-created in this complex time, place, and mix of voices. Our stories are continually informed by these types of varied voices (and more!); portraiture's blend of ethnographic and narrative approaches to research allows researchers to seek out the voices of more than just the participants themselves. This can mean interviewing participants' peers, attending to one's own voice as a researcher, and it could mean recognizing voices in the more-than-human as well (Timmerman & Piersol, 2013).

Multifaceted conceptions of voice have often been used in social science research to *narrow* in on meaning, triangulating between different voices to find the one kernel of truth. However, in portraiture, multifaceted conceptions of voice also increase the ambiguity of experience and expertise, *broadening* notions of what is real and/or important. In a context where it is easy to oversimplify, portraiture's inclusion of multifaceted voices helps preserve the complexity, co-creative, and relational nature of our experiences and ideas.

Finally, portraiture's use of story and literary devices also produces an aesthetic form of knowledge. Lawrence-Lightfoot and Hoffmann Davis (1997) explain that portraits should be literary, artistic, and accessible, using narrative to express "attitudes, feelings, colors, pace, and ambiance" (p. 28). These aesthetic expressions "do more than refer… to the object of representation, their own properties have significance in themselves" (p. 28). Employing metaphor, variations in tone, and intentional use of flow in the portrait gives researchers the ability to express a wider array of information. For example, concepts or experiences that might be otherwise difficult to quantify or evaluate, or are simply ineffable, can be brought to life through story. Their weight, intention, and meaning can be conveyed in the simple description of the brush of a hand, a pause, or a tear rather than attempting to find narrow words for the actual phenomena itself. That is, the aesthetic aspects of portraiture are not merely window-dressing, but are meaningful in and of themselves.

Further, portraiture's use of literary storytelling asserts the value of aesthetic and subjective knowledge. Unashamedly including, and even foregrounding, the otherwise commonly marginalized "evocative, emotional, nonrational, subjective, metaphoric" (Richardson, 1997, p. 39), and sensory qualities of experience, makes an ethical statement about the value of these experiences. "In performing our subjectivities, we assert the relevance, the legitimacy, indeed the necessity of including the full range of our humanness in our work of remembering ourselves in/to the world, embracing the world, with all our relations" (Hasebe-Ludt, Chambers, Oberg, & Leggo, 2008, p. 68).

Tending to Resonance as Validity

Given the focus in portraiture on a complex notion of "goodness," the cultivation of relationship with participants, and forms of analysis and writing that are aesthetic and story-driven, it should be no surprise that portraiture does not use notions of objectivity or generalizability to assess the credibility of research. Instead, one of the key goals of portraiture, and what Lawrence-Lightfoot and Hoffmann Davis (1997) say is an indication of "valid" portraiture, is a portrait that expresses the "authenticity" and "essence" of participants. Even though they fully acknowledge the overwhelming influence of the researcher in shaping the purpose, questions, and representation of the project, their goal is for participants to have a "Yes, that's me!" response when they read the final portraits (p. 247). This goal has been the subject of some critique, as it could suggest some kind of finality to a person, a capital-T "truth," or the sense that people do not change with time and experience (English, 2000; McKenzie, 2006). In my own experiences with portraiture, I often wondered—even if I were to accept the notion that each person has an essence—whether I, as a researcher, would have the capacity to sense, identify, translate, and represent that essence. Thus, in response to these concerns over terms, I interpret Lawrence-Lightfoot and Hoffman Davis' (1997) discussion of "authenticity" and "essence" as a cautionary guideline for researchers. In seeking "authenticity" and "essence," they rightly warn of the potential to create simple (versus complex) portraits and/or portraits that represent the researcher more than the participant.

I found it is possible to take heed of this warning and also avoid essentializing through two equally important processes: 1) establishing practices for the inclusion of ambiguity and multiple "truths" about participants, and 2) establishing a "multi-layered resonance" with portraits. To achieve the former, the inclusion of ambiguity and multiple "truths," it was paramount to understand "goodness" as complex and ambiguous, and create deep relationships with participants so they can express complexity, ambiguity, and vulnerability. Likewise, researchers can also avoid essentializing by understanding storytelling as co-created knowledge and as context-dependent. Thus, in seeking out a kind of validity and authenticity in portraiture, I found it was foundationally important to draw upon the notions of "goodness," relationship, story, and artistry outlined above.

The second process for considering the "validity" of a portrait is tending to a multi-layered resonance. A multi-layered resonance evaluates whether portraits create representations of participants' lives that resonate with participants themselves, with the researcher(s), and with readers (Clandinin, Pushor, & Orr, 2007; Clough, 2002; Hart, 2002). Lawrence-Lightfoot & Hoffmann Davis (1997) write:

> The portraitist hopes to develop a rich portrayal that will have resonance (in different ways, from different perspectives) with three different audiences: with the actors who will see themselves reflected in the story, with the readers who will see no reason to disbelieve it, and with the portraitist herself, whose deep knowledge of the setting and self-critical stance allow her to see the "truth-value" in her work. (p. 247)

First, *resonance for "actors"* refers to the reactions participants have when reading a draft of their own portraits, whether they recognize themselves within them. While a researcher's portrayal will (and should) inevitably look quite different from a participant's own view of self, there is a need to ensure a base level of participant recognition in the work, particularly because portraits are not anonymous and there is thus more potential for harm (Lawrence-Lightfoot and Hoffmann Davis, 1997). Referring to Lincoln (1995), Hart (2002) suggests that researchers might establish "reciprocity (vs. hierarchy)" (p. 151) as one criterion for validity in narrative environmental education research. I see portraiture's desire for resonance with participants as one step in a reciprocal direction rather than a researcher-as-expert-on-others, hierarchical direction.

Second, *resonance for readers* refers to the believability of the portrait for the intended audience. Many narrative and literary arts-based researchers focus on this aspect of validity. Hart (2002) suggests that, "we interpret stories from their verisimilitude, their lifelikeness. … The narrative interest is in whether it is believable" (p. 147). Similarly, Clandinin, Pushor, and Orr (2007) highlight authenticity, adequacy, plausibility, recognizability of the field, and resonance as their criteria for narrative research validity. Resonance in this case means believability, which in turn means understanding, which can then in turn mean change. As Clough (2002) writes, our primary impulse for affirming research is not our assessment of its validity, but is its "ability to speak to our experience… For what is research in educational settings *for* if it is not to *understand*; and when we understand, we can change (Bolton, 1981)" (p. 83). Seeking resonance for readers requires researchers to be aware of their positionality, both in terms of "personal standpoint judgments," and in relation to "specific discourse communities" (i.e. academic fields) (Hart, 2002, p. 151). In other words, for a portrait to resonate with readers, researchers must be self-reflexively aware of how their own standpoint influences their writing in relation to the particular audience likely to read their work.

Building off this self-reflexivity, the third aspect of portraiture validity, *resonance for the portraitist,* describes a process of critical discernment whereby researchers engage in a self-criticism of the portraits, imagining what some of the most salient challenges would be, and working through them (Lawrence-Lightfoot & Hoffmann Davis, 1997). As described above, this kind of resonance requires that researchers examine their own values, assumptions, and privilege (Hart, 2002). Having done so does not imply that they will then be able to take on a more objective or accurate stance, but rather that they can be aware of instances where their own positionality normalizes aspects of the portraits, and accordingly, where others might find room to challenge these same aspects from an alternate position.

At face value, it might seem that these three searches for resonance could lead researchers (consciously or not) to write portraits that aim to please the participants, readers, and portraitists, and use logical, simplistic storylines. Lawrence-Lightfoot and Hoffmann Davis (1997) draw from Miles and Huberman (1984) to describe these problematic tendencies as 1) the "holistic fallacy," a researcher tendency to identify clarity within a storyline, amongst patterns, and/or within data that are otherwise actually incongruent or ambiguous; and 2) the tendency to lose one's own perspective as a researcher, instead being "co-opted into the perceptions and explanations of local informants [p. 263]" (p. 246). To counter these tendencies amongst portraitists, I used Barone's (2001) work, which suggests that literary-style arts-based researchers include stories and themes that highlight ambiguity and complexity in their work to increase its validity (p. 25). Similarly, Richardson's (2000) metaphor of crystallization rather than triangulation for validity can help researchers avoid the tendencies above. She explains, "Crystals grow, change, alter, but are not amorphous. Crystals are prisms that reflect externalities *and* refract within themselves, creating different colors, patterns, and arrays, casting off in different directions" (p. 934). Thus, what makes a portrait valid is its multi-layered resonance—with participants, researchers, and their audience—which includes ambiguity within the writing and an end "product" that, while reflecting what rings true at the time of its writing, is allowed to grow and change with time and interpretation.

In the following sections, I describe how I used portraiture to create the three portraits that ground this book. The writing below thus demonstrates one version of what the visions and aspirations of portraiture outlined above can look like in practice.

Portraiture in Practice

For each portrait, I had three phases of data collection. I began by collecting background ethnographic data. This included many steps: I read my participants' publications; searched online for recognition of their teaching, research, and/or service; gathered information about the institutions where they worked; and learned about the colonial and place-based histories of where they lived. In this initial phase, I also had some phone conversations with participants, starting the work of building trust and understanding between us by getting to know one another and making plans. Next, the bulk of my data gathering occurred during 4–6-day-long site visits with each participant. During these site visits, I conducted three audio-recorded, semi-structured interviews with each participant, as well as having many informal research-related conversations with participants, their friends, family, and colleagues. Participant and nonparticipant observation and experience were key aspects of the site visits, equally if not more important than the interviews because of the insight they provided into what participants actually do (Goetz & LeCompte, 1984). I recorded observations and experiences with field notes (both written and audio), sketches, photographs, and/or found objects (e.g. a few stalks of wheat from the fields where a participant lived). During site visits, participants also shared many documents with me (such as books, articles, and course readers) that I turned to once I got home for further information. After site visits and preliminary analysis, the third phase consisted of follow-up phone interviews with each participant. I had one primary follow-up interview after the site visits and before writing the portraits. Several years later, after completing my dissertation (Timmerman, 2013) and in the process of getting ready to write this book, I had another, lengthier follow-up interview in which we reflected on the portraits created years before. Dialogues from that interview appear at the end of each of the original portraits in this book.

Analysis for this project began during site visits when, at the end of each day, I would reflect upon and analyze emerging trends as well as surprising, "outlying" moments (Lawrence-Lightfoot & Hoffman Davis, 1997). After site visits, I undertook an ethnographic sorting, grouping, and classification of all the information I had gathered (Goetz & LeCompte, 1984). In this phase, I attended to both themes and categories. Themes included emergent ideas or explanations that crossed categorical lines; categories included pre-determined topics or areas of participants' lives that I studied. For example, "food" was a *theme* that emerged in Madhu's portrait across the *categories* of "educational philosophy" and "home life." This sorting, grouping, and classification happened several times for each participant until I felt I had established categories and themes that were sufficiently representative. During each reading/listening/looking, and all together at the end, I searched for *meaningful* (versus simply recurrent) themes. Equally important to the ethnographic sorting, grouping, and classification was an aesthetically driven analysis and writing that paid attention to the flow, feel, and whole of the portrait. This process took much longer and, arguably, included much more "analysis" than did the ethnographically informed aspects. I wrote and re-wrote at least six or seven drafts of each portrait, each time learning and discovering something new about how to frame, understand, compare, and represent what I had experienced and learned with each participant. Richardson (2000) refers to this as *creative analytic practices* in which "the *writing process* and the *writing product* [are] deeply intertwined" (p. 930). During analysis, I attempted to acknowledge and keep intact the "complex interplay of voices" (Lawrence-Lightfoot & Hoffman Davis, 1997, p. 191) by (for example) not reducing contradictory ideas or stories down to one "truth," but rather allowing both versions to exist simultaneously. This practice aligns with Barone's (2001) statement that some research does not aim for one, true answer to the research question, but instead hopes to explore and uncover multiple understandings.

Lawrence-Lightfoot and Hoffmann Davis (1997) use the metaphor of weaving a tapestry to help describe what it is like to create a portrait. They suggest that this metaphor reflects "the elements of structure, texture, color, design, and the images of spinning a tale, telling a story, shaping a narrative" (p. 247). There are four aspects of this kind of weaving: conception, structure, form and cohesion. The *conception* of a portrait is the "overarching story" or organizing "skeleton" of the narrative. It is the first step in transferring the research analysis into a representation, using the most dominant emergent themes to create a vision of the whole. For example, in Madhu's portrait, I used the basket maker story as the overarching narrative to frame her portrait. "If [the first phase of] *conception* [emphasis added] expresses the overarching vision of the aesthetic whole (the tapestry), then the *structure* [emphasis added] represents the warp and weft of the weaving" (p. 252). In this *structure* phase, I brought in the unique themes for each portrait and worked through how those themes would create an internal structure to the overarching arc. Giving form to the structure turns the portrait from an outline into a narrative. Again, Lawrence-Lightfoot and Hoffmann Davis explain, "Form—expressed in stories, examples, illustrations, illusion, ironies— gives life and movement to the narrative, providing complexity, subtlety, and nuance to the text, and offering the reader opportunities for feeling identified and drawn into the piece" (p. 254). Finally, portraitists attend to coherence. Partly out of an effective combination of the first three steps, and partly out of a final look at the piece as a whole, researchers create coherence by ensuring that the portrait flows, has consistency in the writer's voice, and the parts fit together as a whole.

Challenges and Limitations of Using Portraiture

My practice to find a "multi-layered resonance" included creating many versions of each portrait and sharing selected versions of those first with my advisors. These multiple versions and readings gave me space from my writing to evaluate it for "resonance," something that was otherwise difficult to assess when I was too close and attached to one particular version of the story I was writing.

The portraits also went through multiple sets of reviews by both participants and anyone else who was mentioned by name and/or quoted within the portrait. Once I had a solid first draft that had been reviewed by my doctoral dissertation advisors, I contacted participants' friends, colleagues, and/or students who were mentioned by name within my portrait drafts. For example, in David's portrait, there is a section where I describe a conversation between David and two of his former students, Francene and Justin. I asked them, and all others mentioned by name in the participants' portraits, to review only the section of the portrait that corresponded to their contribution. I received these approvals before sending drafts of the whole portraits to participants. It was important to me that my participants' colleagues reviewed their contributions first because I wanted to ensure that they felt alignment with how they were represented before I shared those representations with their colleague/friend/professor. This helped to avoid indirect or triangular communication.

Each participant also reviewed drafts of their respective portraits. Following the advice of Jessica Hoffmann Davis (personal communication, February 2013), I gave my participants two opportunities for feedback on the original portraits that I wrote of them. First, I sought substantive, major feedback on their portraits. It was difficult. I broke down in tears on a phone call with Madhu discussing how I had interpreted some things she had said in the wrong way and thus represented her feelings incorrectly. It felt so difficult because my sense of reciprocity and the depth of our relationship was so substantial; she trusted me and I respected her, and the responsibility of creating a portrait that held resonance for her was something I deeply felt. Moreover, there was a "junior-senior" dynamic at play, given my status as a PhD student researching three respected professors. After completing this substantive round of feedback with all three of my original research participants for their portraits, the second round was a fact-checking, editorial review at the end of the writing process. Jessica Hoffmann Davis suggested limiting participant edits to these two rounds because it would be easy to otherwise end up in a cycle of revisions that attempted to erase the portraitist's presence. She argued, and I agreed, that the portraits are ultimately created by researchers, and while they ought to resonate with participants, they are not self-portraits.

While writing the portraits, one of my most salient challenges emerged when the story I saw was different from the story I was told. Particularly interested in notions of contradiction and complicity, yet also seeking out trusting relationships, I sometimes felt I was in a bind, unsure of whether to pursue the contradictions, trusting my "outsider eyes" over the stories told and emphasized by participants. As I created the portraits, I dealt with this difficulty by inserting my own voice into the text in these instances of confusion or contradiction. Rather than presume I knew best by telling the story that I saw over the story that I heard, I chose to share with readers my personal thoughts and challenges. This enabled me to bring the confusion and contradiction I saw into view without compromising participants' stories and trust.

Other challenges and limitations I faced through my use of portraiture primarily centered around scope and inclusion. I had hoped to have participants from both Canada and the US and to have a more racially diverse group, but in the complex mix of identifying who, with the right disciplinary focus, in what geographic area, was available when, it proved impossible to meet all my ideals of participant diversity. This is one of the reasons why I chose to bring other voices into this book with the inclusion of the vignettes. I also wish I would have had two to three site visits with each participant and more interactions with their colleagues and places to create more in-depth portraits. Finally, though this research expresses the importance of relationships with human and ecological communities, it is undoubtedly focused on individuals. I noticed this limitation in my visit with Ray where my questions about *one's* ecological philosophy and *one's* personal and professional practice juxtaposed with his philosophy and practice that is held more among a people or a community. In future work, I am interested in exploring portraiture that has groups or communities as its focus, rather than individuals (e.g. Pickeral, Hill, & Duckenfield, 2003; Davis, Soep, Maira, Remba, & Putnoi, 1993).

Portraiture was an incredibly rewarding research methodology. It led me to befriending three amazing educators, the writing process was creative yet rigorous, and the orientation toward learning and deeply questioning goodness has given me inspiration.

Note

1 Aspects of this chapter previously appeared in a book chapter I wrote titled "Relationship, complexity, and co-creation in portraiture research" in Blenkinsop, Fettes, & Piersol's 2022 Edited book, *Ecoportraiture in education: Learning and storying with the more-than-human* (Timmerman, 2022).

References

Bailey, L. E. (2012). Feminist research. In S. D. Lapan, M. T. Quartaroli, & F. J. Reimer (Eds.), *Qualitative research: An introduction to methods and designs* (pp. 391–422). Jossey-Bass.

Barone, T. (2000). *Aesthetics, politics, and educational inquiry: Essays and examples.* Peter Lang.

Barone, T. (2001). Science, art, and the predispositions of educational researchers. *Educational Researcher, 30*(7), 24–28.

Blenkinsop, S., Fettes, M., & Piersol, L. (Eds.) (2022). *Ecoportraiture in education: Learning and storying with the more-than-human.* Peter Lang.

Castagno, A. (2012). What makes critical ethnography "critical"? In S. D. Lapan, M. T. Quartaroli, & F. J. Reimer (Eds.), *Qualitative research: An introduction to methods and designs* (pp. 373–390). Jossey-Bass.

Cheney, J. (1989). Postmodern environmental ethics: Ethics as bioregional narrative. *Environmental Ethics, 11,* 117–134.

Clandinin, D. J., Pushor, D., & Orr, A. M. (2007). Navigating sites for narrative inquiry. *Journal of Teacher Education, 58*(21), 21–35.

Clough, P. (2002). *Narratives and fictions in educational research.* Open University Press.

Davis, J., Soep, E., Maira, S., Remba, N., & Putnoi, D. (1993). *Safe havens: Portraits of educational effectiveness in community art centers that focus on education in economically disadvantaged communities.* Harvard Project Zero, Harvard University.

Eisner, E. (1997). The promise and perils of alternative forms of data representation. *Educational Researcher, 26*(6), 4–9.

English, F. W. (2000). A critical appraisal of Sara Lawrence-Lightfoot's portraiture as a method of educational research. *Educational Researcher, 29*(7), 21–26.

Fawcett, L. (2000). Ethical imagining: Ecofeminist possibilities and environmental learning. *Canadian Journal of Environmental Education, 5*, 134–149.

Gaard, G. (2009). Children's environmental literature: From ecocriticism to ecopedagogy. *Neohelicon, 36*, 321–334.

Goetz, J., & LeCompte, M. (1984). *Ethnography and qualitative design in educational research.* Academic Press.

Gough, A. (1999). Recognizing women in environmental education pedagogy and research. *Environmental Education Research, 5*(2), 143–161.

Hallen, P. (2000). Ecofeminism goes bush. *Canadian Journal of Environmental Education, 5*, 150–166.

Hart, P. (2002). Narrative, knowing, and emerging methodologies in environmental education research: Issues of quality. *Canadian Journal of Environmental Education, 7*(2), 140–165.

Harvester, L., & Blenkinsop, S. (2010). Environmental education and ecofeminist pedagogy: Bridging the environmental and the social. *Canadian Journal of Environmental Education, 15*, 120–134.

Hasebe-Ludt, E., Chambers, C., Oberg, A., & Leggo, C. (2008). Embracing the world, eith all our relations: Métissage as an artful braiding. In S. Springgay, R. Irwin, C. Leggo, & P. Gouzouasis (Eds.), *Being with A/r/tography* (pp. 57–68). Sense Publishers.

Kim, J. H. (2016). *Understanding narrative inquiry: The crafting and analysis of stories as research.* Sage Publications.

Lawrence-Lightfoot, S., & Hoffmann Davis, J. (1997). *The art and science of portraiture.* Jossey-Bass.

Lemley, C., & Mitchell, R. W. (2012). Narrative inquiry: Stories lived, stories told. In S. D. Lapan, M. T. Quartaroli, & F. J. Reimer (Eds.), *Qualitative research: An introduction to methods and designs* (pp. 215–242). Jossey-Bass.

Lincoln, Y. S. (1995). Emerging criteria for quality in qualitative interpretive research. *Qualitative Inquiry, 1*(3), 275–289.

McKenzie, M. (2006). Three portraits of resistance: The (un)making of Canadian students. *Canadian Journal of Education, 29*(1), 199–222.

Miles, M. B., & Huberman, A. M. (1984). Drawing Valid Meaning from Qualitative Data: Toward a Shared Craft. *Educational Researcher, 13*(5), 20–30. https://doi.org/10.3102/0013189X013005020

Pickeral, T., Hill, D., & Duckenfield, M. (2003). The promise and challenge of service-learning portraiture research. In S. H. Billig & A. S. Waterman (Eds.), *Studying service-learning: Innovations in education research methodology* (pp. 207–222). Lawrence Erlbaum Associates.

Piersol, L., & Timmerman, N. (2017). Reimagining environmental education within academia: Storytelling and dialogue as lived ecofeminist politics. *Journal of Environmental Education, 48*(1), 10–17. DOI: 10.1080/00958964.2016.1249329

Profeit-LeBlanc, L. (2002). Four faces of story. *Canadian Journal of Environmental Education, 7*(2), 47–53.

Reimer, F. (2012). Ethnographic research. In S. D. Lapan, M. T. Quartaroli, & F. J. Reimer (Eds.), *Qualitative research: An introduction to methods and designs* (pp. 163–188). Jossey-Bass.

Richardson, L. (1997). *Fields of play: Constructing an academic life*. Rutgers University Press.

Richardson, L. (2000). Writing: A method of inquiry. In N. K. Denzin & Y. S. Lincoln (Eds.), *Handbook of qualitative research methods* (pp. 923–948). Sage Publications.

Russell, C., & Bell, A. C. (1996). A politicized ethic of care: Environmental education from an ecofeminist perspective. *Women's Voices in Experiential Education, 21,* 172–181.

Timmerman, N. (2013). *Coherence, consistency, contradiction: Portraits of post-secondary educators seeking integrity*. Unpublished Doctoral Dissertation, UBC.

Timmerman, N., & Piersol, L. (2013, June). *Storied sketches of people and place: Portraiture in environmental education research*. Paper presented at the Canadian Society for Studies of Education, Victoria, BC.

Timmerman, N. (2022). Relationship, complexity, and co-creation in portraiture research. In S. Blenkinsop, M. Fettes, & L. Piersol (Eds.), *Ecoportraiture in education: Learning and storying with the more-than-human*. Peter Lang.

Part II
Storying

Stories make up the heart of this book. In this section, you will find three portraits and nine vignettes. I wrote the three portraits first, added the abridged dialogues that appear at the end of those portraits a few years later, and the vignettes were written by educators themselves with my editorial guidance. Generously woven through all these stories are vulnerable, courageous, unsure, and curious words. Each of the educators highlighted here shared their stories at different moments in their lives. Some were close to retirement, others newly embarking on teaching. Some were on sabbatical with time to rest and reflect, others were preparing for teaching courses of 200 students. As you read the next several chapters, I ask that you extend generosity to the complexity of each educator's context and how it shapes the specific stories and insights they brought to the forefront, knowing there are so many more stories and insights that have gone unwritten. Please also respect the vulnerability these educators show by sharing their questions and convictions. And for the portraits especially, remember that the framing, sorting, and selecting of these stories ultimately lies with me, rendering any inaccuracy my own, not theirs.

3

David Greenwood

A Faustian Bargain

A short three-minute walk up the country road in front of David Greenwood's house brings us to Greenwood Cemetery (no relation) in Palouse, Washington. Continuing only one minute more would take us to the wheat fields. Before we get to the wheat and turn onto the winding road that skirts the Palouse River, David walks up to a gravestone. It is simple: gray, rectangular, horizontally set, typical at first sight. As I read the epitaph for the second time, however, I puzzle over its meaning. "Victim of corporation greed," it says. Recalling the details from a local, historical publication, David shares the story…

In the early 1900s, Palouse was the hub of logging, mining, and railroad industries working as fast as they could to make as much money as they could from the land. Yet, these industries were starting to dry up and the economy was shifting to agriculture. As businesses fought to stay alive, they scraped corners, overworked employees, and became lax on safety regulations. The man whose grave we stood upon worked for Northern Pacific Railroad. One day, while filling an oil can near the repair tracks, a "door from a ballast car swung out and caught young Brown, crushing him against the building where he was at work, breaking the pelvis bone and inflicting internal injuries" (Kiessling, 1999, p. 23).

36 | *Between Complicity and Integrity*

Figure 3.1. Victim of Corporation Greed
Source: Author.

Especially tragic as he had only a few days prior decided to "take up some less hazardous line of work" (p. 24) in light of his upcoming marriage, Bert Leon Brown died at age 24 of internal trauma, "victim of corporation greed." His parents, who had just barely made it to the hospital to spend his last 40 minutes of life with him, were irate with the injustice of their son's death and chose these words to adorn his gravestone lest the people of the Palouse forget.

As David finishes telling Bert's story, he tells me that working in the university sometimes feels like working in a corporation. Even alongside the many privileges and freedoms that come with being a professor of education, one can also feel a "victim of corporation greed." This feeling is a microcosm of the larger context of today's world, of the primacy of corporate power over people and land. All life (humans, forests, birds, frogs, rivers, the Earth itself) is a "victim of corporation greed," albeit differentially along lines of privilege. Prioritizing output over worker safety, Bert's death is symptomatic of a culture of colonization and neoliberal capitalism, a culture of what, in reference to Hardt and Negri's (2000) work, David calls "empire" (2010b). Empire is the worldwide "bio-political power" (p. 14) that demands conformity to a neo-corporate economy, shapes human and nonhuman lives around productivity, organizes individuals and collectives through domination and hierarchy, and arrests the vibrant diversity of cultures and languages that have heretofore characterized human community on Earth. In the wake of empire are countless victims, some significantly worse off than others and/or more complicit than others. David offers a quote from Wendell Berry (2012) in agreement that empire is "indifferent… It [does] not *intend* to victimize its victims. It simply follow[s] its single purpose of the highest possible profit, and ignore[s] the 'side effects'" (para. 21).

Talking and walking together this fall morning, I am struck by the depth and detail of David's historical knowledge of this particular place and how it is connected to the larger forces of empire. His care for and awareness of the stories of Palouse seem to suggest that his family has been living there for generations rather than six years. And, David is clearly a reflective, thoughtful person, attuned to how the personal choices and circumstances of his life's path are contextualized within larger socio-cultural and political powers. I was pleased with his openness and honesty about the complexities, uncertainties, vulnerability, and frustration of this time in his life. With questions about integrity and complicity on my mind as a researcher, I felt assured from this early conversation that we would traverse rich terrain in our talks and walks together.

I encountered David on a section of his life's path that was the "calm before the storm" of a significant life transition. Professionally, he was shifting from an Associate Professor position at Washington State University, where he had been for seven years, to a new position as Canada Research Chair in Environmental Education at Lakehead University.[1] Personally, the move from Palouse, Washington to Thunder Bay, Ontario saw his family of five riding an emotional rollercoaster as they worked through the uprooting of patterns and ties to one place, and the search for opportunities to fill them in another.

When planning my visit, David suggested we should "be spontaneous… just hang out and be challenged." Despite not overly planning our time together, David generously and carefully thought out several appropriate places to visit, people to meet, and walks to be had, the first of which was our visit to Bert's gravestone. The story of Bert's unfortunate death offered a frame through which we explored David's perspectives on socio-ecological "victimization," and "corporate greed," as well as his sense of personal complicity and resistance therein. Fully acknowledging how educational institutions contribute to socio-ecological injustices, David has understandably mixed feelings about his work. On one hand, he says, it's the greatest job ever, but on the other, it's the Faustian bargain, it's like you're selling your soul at the crossroads.

Confronting Empire's Education

Like Bert's working conditions, David identifies how institutions of education are also often dictated by the powers and goals of empire. David thus critiques dominant curricular and pedagogical approaches on many accounts. He suggests that there is a significant disconnect between what students experience and where meaning is held inside versus outside of school, between the everyday experiences of family, friendship, and place-based meaning, and the abstracted, reductionistic, and—frankly—boring curricula and pedagogy of most educational operations. Institutionalized education functions as if it were floating above places, disconnected and ambivalent to what happened there previously, what is happening there now, and what should happen there in the future (Gruenewald, 2008). He writes, "The home world of meaning, relevance, and nurturance is exchanged for an alien, mechanical environment that fails to connect, fails to acknowledge what is missing, and, what is worse, destroys the child's ability to reenter the world of meaning left behind" (Gruenewald,[2] 2003b, p. 292). That is, the classroom becomes a space that is glorified as the epicenter of learning, the locus for the latest pedagogical fad, yet it remains a sterile box devoid of contact and actual "experience with the 'mystical moist' stuff of life" (p. 281).

Part of the lack of contact with the "mystical moist stuff of life" comes from schooling largely taking place indoors, what David also critiques as an "egregious absence of contact with the land from dominant educational discourses and practices" (Gruenewald, 2003a, p. 41). Even more subtly, though, it is not only the enclosure of bodies indoors, but it is the emphasis on so-called "measurable," standardized knowledge that works away at erasing the importance of the ambiguous, immeasurable aspects of relationships to place and the more-than-human. In an essay called *Resistance, Reinhabitation, and Regime Change*, David says "Ivan Illich wrote, 'People who have been schooled down to size let unmeasured experience slip out of their hands.'" (Gruenewald, 2006, p. 3). Thus, David feels that some of the primary work critical, place-based educators must do is to resist the erasure of unmeasured experience. In other words, resist the notion that learning and knowledge is only valuable when it can be measured. On the contrary, our relationships to one another, our communities, the land, and the narratives that bind us in wholesome relationships to one another are difficult to "measure" by any text, quiz, or term paper, but remain the most essential knowledge for sustaining people and place.

Figure 3.2. The Mystical Moist Night Air
In several publications, David illustrates schools' "enclosure of bodies" with Whitman's poem "When I heard the learn'd astronomer:"
When I heard the learn'd astronomer,
When the proofs, the figures, were ranged in columns before me,
When I was shown the charts and diagrams, to add, divide and measure them,
When I sitting heard the astronomer where he lectured with much applause in the lecture-room,
How soon unaccountable I became tired and sick,
Till rising and gliding out I wander'd off by myself,
In the mystical moist night-air, and from time to time,
Look'd up in perfect silence at the stars. (Whitman, 1993, p. 340)
Source: Author.

David and I discuss his experience of these critiques—as someone who finds himself both resisting and reinscribing them. He begins by recognizing the relatively mild nature of the hardships and frustrations he experiences, given his privileged location as a middle-class, white, heterosexual man. And, he does not shy away from acknowledging his complicity in reproducing problematic institutional norms. He expresses both sadness and anger at how education's enclosures, abstractions, and assimilations generally "conspire against the human soul, or even the *idea* of a human soul," how [they are] destructive to our bodies and spirits, "reshap[ing] humans as machines." Considering these statements personally, David talks through his own experience of being emotionally and physiologically drained by enclosures of his body and thoughts. Even as we sit inside the space of his backyard office—a rare moment inside compared to most of our outdoor wanderings—the window is cracked and he tells me how he will always try to open a window in any indoor space. "*I NEED AIR.* No matter where I am, I have this need to just open the fucking window!"

Further, David links the aspects of how institutions end up "taking away [one's] sense of self" to other "institutional dynamics [that are] so geared toward productivity and so not-geared toward nurturing the whole person… or for that matter, the community or the land." In his experience, the pressure to perform and produce not only affects his own sense of self, but also disrupts his relationships with others. He describes a conversation he had with a colleague who said, "All academics I know are workaholics." David says it's true, but that he does not want to be one: "My father was and… even though I resented him, I hated him for it, I became him. Classic family dynamics. I have been a workaholic in the last ten years—not the last few—after I got tenure, I started to be in recovery." Feeling as if he needed to "overachieve" in order to be "safe," David experienced the over-expenditure of "time and energy and the costs associated to family and self and to others." Even now, in this time of "recovery," the transition that he and his family are experiencing in the move from Palouse to Thunder Bay, has resulted in an "amazing amount of grief and stress." For a family of place-based educators and children who have grown up in close connection with the land on which they live, the reality of moving and uprooting for a job is particularly difficult to reconcile.

Standing a few paces away from Bert Brown's grave, we walk under the swaying branches of a giant willow, the cemetery's United States' flag catches the wind, and its attached rope clangs against the pole. "So, why do you do it, then?" I ask. Given your sense of corporate greed alive and well within the postsecondary institutions you work for, of the ways in which those systems perpetuate colonial, neoliberal norms and prioritize learning you don't believe in, why choose to work within such a system? Initially, David answers by reiterating the privilege of his job: "It's the most privileged job in the world. I get to think, reflect, and write, and I get paid a lot of money to do it." I ask him whether it would be possible to

Figure 3.3. Collected Nests
Also a place-based educator, David's partner, Jill Addington Greenwood, homeschools their three children: eldest Eli, and twins, Kate and Ivy. I am introduced to them as they bake with local pumpkins, I see their morning routine of collecting chicken eggs, and we get to know one another over an evening board game. Yet, amongst these place-centric activities, the giddy chirps of Hanna Montana flickering on the evening TV are making more of an appearance than normal during my visit, as they cope with the stress of their upcoming move.
Source: Author.

engage in these same kinds of activities, but outside of the context of a university. In response, he recounts a time in which he lived off the land and, yes, was able to do much of the same thinking, reflecting, and writing outside of the institution. However, he did it for little or no money. And once his family came, so did a sense of responsibility to engage within a social system that would allow for them to have choices and opportunities down the road. It is a reality that I rarely hear academics acknowledge, but having a regular salary and support for yourself and/or family does matter.

In later conversations, another significant reason for David's choice to work as an academic emerges, which is his desire to "be a part of social change." Many educators feel this call. For David, he describes working for social change as both a privilege and a responsibility.

He explains that the roots of his desire to work toward social change come from being an "on-the-margins" kind of kid, one who worked at trying to conform for some time before he grew to realize that the search for conformity was unfulfilling. In high school, after reading Thoreau, he became happier being on the margins and instead found himself largely discontented with the "BS of society." These days, David continues to turn to Thoreau and works toward social change alongside acknowledgments of his own complicity. He writes,

> My own uneasy relationship with the teacher education bureaucracy is nicely captured by Thoreau (1947, p. 609) in his observations of the culture of his time: 'The greater part of what my neighbors call good,' Thoreau wrote, 'I believe in my soul to be bad, and if I repent of anything, it is my good behavior.' I likewise repent at my own many compromises of conformity to a regulated system that has little to do with what I truly value. (Greenwood, 2010a, p. 5)

In some instances, David's feelings about his choice to work as a professor are heavier than others. While he enjoys the privileges and much of the work expected of him, he also refers to his sense of complicity within postsecondary institutions as a "Faustian bargain," a "selling of [his] soul at the crossroads." In reconciling the privileges and complicity, David sometimes aims for a sense of balance. He describes how he tries to "achieve goals and meet expectations without entering into a Faustian Bargain where the costs start to mount… it's my own integrity, it's my health, it's my relationships… as much as possible I want to live outside that game and just be real." But when it comes down to it, that balance—if and when it does appear—is fleeting.

Accordingly, David negotiates his privileges and complicity by embracing a sense of struggle. In response to a question I have about times when he felt good about his work, he ends up suggesting that he feels best when fully engaged within the struggle: "I don't really feel I have a finest hour as a professional… I've struggled a lot, you know? And, my finest hours are probably within that struggle, right? I mean, that's what it's about for me. The struggle is where the windows and doors open and it's the little glimpses of what you might make happen, even within the struggle, that sustain me. But, you know, the finest hour is yet to come. All my songs are redemption songs. I'm not the shining example."

A Walk

Rounding the hill, we walk down onto a road covered in gravel, black and wet with recent rain. We walk mostly silently, save for the gritty crunch of one foot placed in front of the other. After several minutes, David veers off to the left toward the trees. Following his silent lead, our footsteps become quiet as the coarse gravel gives way to a soft bed of ponderosa pine needles. As the ground begins to tilt down toward the Palouse River and we duck under the first of many low-hanging branches, I notice David has stopped. With a joyful fire in his blue, blue eyes, he turns to say in a hushed and excited voice, "I like to walk where the deer walk."

When it comes to the beauty of a place and being with the land, David does not hesitate to speak with reverence, many pauses, a tear, or hearty laughter. As we walk, he begins to share aspects of his ecological philosophy with me. He uses the phrase "the land" often as he talks and I ask him to clarify what that means to him. "The land is everything, I mean, the land *is* us, … there is no other place." David also says, smiling, "I am *mad* for it to be in contact with me" (Whitman, 1892, para. 6). A favorite Walt Whitman quote, this passage captures David's itching need to connect with the land. Walks such as the one we are taking now are "sacred." They are opportunities to "re-member" himself, his body, with/in the land. Walking provides an opportunity to remember one's membership with/in the land. Clearing his head, getting out of his mind and into his body, David can re-member what he calls (after Thoreau) his *whole* self.

Approaching the river, the undergrowth thickens and we pause, silently observing this place. David spots a kingfisher, our breathing slows to a resting pace, and bit-by-bit, we pick up the conversation. We talk about freedom and wildness. "I have a pretty big… appetite for freedom and wildness," he says. Being outside, something "switches on" inside him; he feels free from institutional constraints that limit behavior, thoughts, and bodies. Wildness, he says, is the freedom to be self-willed, the freedom and spontaneity that come when he can make his own decisions about where to go next. "Nothing makes me feel more present, awake, tuned in, than walking the land and reading the signs, reading the landscape."

On most days, within ten minutes of waking, David is out the door walking. After climbing a nearby hill with views to the Idaho forest or a downhill walk to the Palouse River, he returns home to make tea and toast, settling in with a book for a deep read. He tells me, "The ideal day involves a good walk and a good read. And if I have those things, I feel like I can do anything, pretty much. … Because each of these is an expression of my own freedom and wildness. I choose where to go, I choose what to read. … I feel like I'm growing from each, I feel like I'm being worthwhile." Daily practices of walking and reading enable two types of learning—"one is more accidental and one is more intentional"—and together constitute what Emerson says you need to do to be a learner, and what David likewise takes up as his educational philosophy: "study nature and read books."

In this instance and others, much of David's ecological and educational philosophy draws from romantic and transcendentalist thought, the Anglo-American nature and wilderness tradition. However, as he later tells me—once we have finished our walk through the woods and sit down to some tea and toast—he was also influenced by a mentor—Michael Morris—who "expand[ed] that landscape to include culture and politics."

The language David uses to express his vision for education is thus evocative of the intimate and complex connections between culture, place, politics, and ecology. The words he chooses to express this vision: decolonization and reinhabitation. He describes decolonization as the problematizing of "the *colonization* of people *and* land, both as historical practice and as the political progenitor of today's empire" (Greenwood, 2010b, p. 19). And reinhabitation as "maintaining, restoring, and creating ways of living that are more in tune… [that do] not harm other people and places" (p. 19). Although the work of decolonization and reinhabitation promises to include deep, hard work for individuals, for classrooms, and institutions, when we talk about it, there is an air of excitement in David's voice. I get the sense that his conception of decolonization and reinhabitation focuses on creativity and possibility. Within the process of educating oneself about "the history of colonization of people and land," and how to "develop communities of congruence and resistance," David asserts that there are ample "opportunities for creative work… restoration, and transformation." It is a compelling vision of what education can be.

Alongside this curricular vision for education, David holds a pedagogical one that is context-dependent. He suggests that his responsibility as instructor is to encourage a process of learning in which "people are challenged to articulate who they are, what they want, and are supported in some way to move toward their own ideals." He says, "I believe that we all have something unique to offer a community of others and that part of the role of education ought to be to listen for, identify, nurture, what that gift is." In other words, just as he was inspired by his mentor to "continue to articulate, refine, and nurture, incubate" his own vision "in the presence of others who have diverse yet overlapping visions," he wants to create a pedagogical environment that will encourage others to do the same.

Within these broad frames for curriculum and pedagogy, David asserts that the specific what, why, and how of an educational experience depends upon the people, the place, and the time. When I ask him to describe an educational experience where he walked away thinking, "That was it! That's what I want," he responded accordingly: "It depends on what context we're talking about, right? And then, whatever that was, I would always bring it into the context of place, region, and planet." In this way, his version of context always, already carries with it an ecological dimension, as opposed to some other perspectives that might solely focus on socio-cultural aspects of context. Rounding off our morning's conversation that has meandered through freedom and wildness, vision, and context, David summarizes: "Education for me [is] not just about human being exploration, it's about human being exploration in a context, and that context has an ecological dimension that needs to be understood and explored, and then *the relationship has to be*—ideally, for me, a relationship needs to be developed between the human becoming and the becoming of the place. And, if that's in harmony, then everything's cool!"

Stay Calm. Be Brave. Wait for the Signs.

Mid-morning the next day, we meet with two of David's former graduate students, and I am given some insight into how he integrates notions of trust, spontaneity, vision, context, decolonization, and reinhabitation into a pedagogical practice. During the half-hour drive from David's home to the WSU garden, the land rolls along, giving us alternating views of expansive wheat fields and far-off buttes dark with high desert forests. Nearing the university, but before the characteristic red-brick buildings, we follow a winding road through apple orchards to the top of a hill. Stepping out of the car and around a stand of apple trees, I look down upon a soft slope thick with corn, cabbages, tomatoes, artichokes, eggplant, squash, pumpkins, flowers, beans, culinary herbs, and more. We are greeted first by Justin, who hands us several golden, tiny tomatoes. Delicious. An absolutely perfect blend of mellow sweet and tang brightens my senses and leaves me already grateful to both him and Francene, who have agreed to me sitting in on their meeting with David.

In preparing for this meeting, David describes it as a chance to check in with two people that are "continuing the work" he was part of at WSU. He has no specific agenda, but rather trusts that what needs to be said and discussed will arise on its own. Neither Justin nor Francene are current students of David's—Justin finished his PhD, and Francene has another supervisor—nevertheless, he remains closely tied to their academic and personal journeys. My impression is that this is primarily because they have become friends. Through serendipitous encounters and enough time spent together, David considers Justin "a brother" and Francene "a soul mate for sure." Gathering to talk is partly about catching up on one another's lives, but also, he describes their meetings as "inspiring and conspiring together." Reflecting his previously described educational philosophy, this "inspiring and conspiring" is a process of exploring and creating a personal and collective vision grounded within a place.

Shortly after introductions and hugs are exchanged, David shares a phrase he recently learned from a friend, who had herself reportedly learned it from a Maori friend: "Stay calm. Be brave. Wait for the signs." This mantra strikes him as one to live by and has particular resonance for Francene as well. She repeats it many times and says she likes it. Later in the conversation, as she shuffles through an assortment of ideas for her thesis work, using David and Justin as a sounding board, the sun suddenly comes out and shines down upon us. As it does, she invokes the mantra: "See! Look for the signs! That's my sign. Okay, I think I might do this."

That Francene is entirely serious in this moment, that she feels the first soft rays of sun on her back, turns to watch as a cloud moves to fully reveal its light, and jumping up and down a bit, says with excitement, "hey, these are the signs!," brings me mixed feelings. Initially, I am surprised, my deeply rooted skepticism about cultural appropriation and/or such direct communication between human and all our relations in full swing. Yet, I subsequently adjust toward a sense of observation and seeking understanding. Rather than adopting my own ready-at-hand critiques, Francene demonstrates an openness to the mystery and subjectivity of place. This mystery and subjectivity feels closer to the surface throughout Francene, Justin, and David's meeting in the garden. And, they seem able to find it while simultaneously making way for critical socio-cultural discussions and also localized, particular stories of the history of this place and the people who live(d) here.

Standing adjacent to the sprawling squash, conversation meanders from Francene's thesis topic to departmental culture, faculty interest in place-based initiatives, and a fascinating course that examines Palouse water issues from multiple perspectives. Their academic talk has an air of exuberance, trust, inspiration, and grit. Grounded in story, in place, in communities, it is about who is there, what is happening, what is important, and where people are making meaning. Critical theories emerge as frameworks for understanding these grounded stories and places of meaning. As Francene and Justin talk through their ideas and experiences, David listens a lot. He flows from their enthusiasm into suggestions for future work, encouragements, and probes for deeper understanding of both past experience and future vision.

As the conversation winds its way to a close, we walk up to the tomato bushes. Hungry after almost two hours of talking, I eat at least a dozen of the culls, maybe two. They are even more amazing the second time around. David and I return to his car and to Palouse, and I am left with the slightly sticky, prickly green smell of tomato vines on my hands and a curious mantra in my mind: "Stay calm. Be brave. Wait for the signs."

Navigating Integrity and Complicity—Diving into Paradox

We are walking again. This time, we're walking up, hiking. David's hand reaches out periodically to brush by or lightly grasp the ocean spray, the ponderosa pine, snowberry, and others. Eventually emerging from the trees onto the exposed rock at the top, we are greeted by big sky and big land. Several hawks circle above and the fields are gold with fall crops. Periodically standing, resting, listening, watching, and talking, this is where we have our last interview. The audiotape records almost as many silences as it does conversation, and is dotted with hawk cries and gusty winds throughout.

David brings up the importance of the notion of paradox. He has written about it in publications and discussed it in several conversations during my visit. He explains that, for him, paradox is really a unifying concept, something that brings things together that otherwise do not seem to fit or belong. It is a term he uses to make sense of the experience of complicity and integrity in various contexts. Referring to the field of environmental education, David gives the example of how institutions and critics of them can be united if we consider them as parts of paradox. That is, an institution and the critics of it are paradoxically related because they depend on one another even while the institution exploits its workers and its workers resent and rebel against the institution. This is not to say that the concept of paradox neutralizes the ethical implications of a given paradoxical relationship, but is rather to say that a resolution of the complicity within the relationship is not possible, it is to say that we exist in contradiction. Echoing his earlier inclination to embrace struggle, he says that "going into paradox is the most generative. ... It helps you to ask questions and make discoveries that wouldn't happen otherwise."

The notion of paradox and its associated utility is in service to his desire to see and be a part of substantive social change. Discussing this further atop Kamiak, David explains what social change means to him now, and what it might mean when he transitions to Lakehead University. In terms of research, he has a proposal underway with colleagues that aims to critically analyze what is left out of sustainability discourses in education. This project works toward social change by first allying with a large and potentially powerful social movement toward "sustainability;" and, second, by seeking to deepen and strengthen that movement itself. Despite the disagreement around what sustainability is, David feels that it has momentum, and as long as the discourses can avoid getting too far away from our ecological connections, the differences in opinion around sustainability can be fruitful. It is that idea of paradox again, he says. Uniting the differences through paradox allows for acknowledgment of tension and contradiction while still moving toward social change collectively. Essential to allying with a movement and using that movement to create change is the practice of "partnership, solidarity, and persistence;" we cannot resist empire and "reinhabit our colonized places and lives" without doing so together (Greenwood, 2010b, p. 21).

Continuing the discussion on social change, David explains that a second vision he holds for his future at Lakehead University is to "develop relationships with learning sites that can be used across faculties." He continues, "I really think that all schools and all universities ought to better connect with the land and the sustainability issues in their immediate region. So, how to do this? Well, one way might be to identify a set of exemplary places where people are doing work around sustainability and then develop ways of integrating lots of different courses and programs with those places and the people who know them and work with them."

Of course, one of the challenges most often cited with academic work that engages meaningfully with community partners is that it takes more time. "If you look at faculty members that do a lot of community work, they tend not to have a lot of publications and vice versa." The same is true for engaging students outdoors, David says. He has made sure that there are out-of-doors components to all of his classes, trying "to get outside as much as possible" and give his pre-service teacher education "students a taste of a practice that they could include for themselves if they find rewarding reflection happening there." However, the increasingly strong push toward productivity is not only placed on the shoulders of professors, but it lands on students as well, making "outdoor work ... harder and harder to make time for."

After a lengthy pause in our conversation, I recall how David's desire for social change is connected to his reading of Thoreau (Gruenewald, 2002; Greenwood & McKenzie, 2009), and I ask him, "What does the civil disobedience of an academic look like? ... Not just an academic, but a place-based academic?" Another long pause follows as he mulls the question over. Ideas and answers are tossed about over the next few minutes, and David's thoughts seem to trace two paths. The first has to do with "taking some form of direct action, ... not buying in to the productivity discourse," saying "'No, I'm not going to do that,' and being willing to face consequences." However, he explains, "There's civil disobedience, and then there's being an agent of change—and sometimes they overlap, and sometimes they're separate projects."

Returning to Thoreau, David maps out the ways in which writing—a common "outcome" of the academic push for productivity, and the second path he discusses—can actually be a powerful source of social change. "I think that's one way, is in writing, which is of course, what Thoreau's (1993) *Civil Disobedience* essay was. His act meant nothing, it was the writing of it that became a movement, and one that's been taken up by lots of groups on the ground in lots of different places, so there's definitely value in that." And, ironically, "The good thing about academe is that if you couch your discourse in academic language, you can be pretty radical. ... I've been very critical of the very institution that pays my bills... in an effort to help create an environment that feels more sustainable, more in tune with people, place, and land."

While David has not written a book that has received attention in the way Thoreau's (1993) *Civil Disobedience* has, the 2003 "Critical Pedagogy of Place" article he wrote for *Educational Researcher* (Gruenewald, 2003c) continues to be a reference point for many scholars—critics and fans alike. Indeed, David's publishing record is substantial, not only in terms of its volume, but in terms of its scope and effects. Many environmental educators know his name and reference his poignant writing. Having worked for years in public schools as an English teacher, his talent for crafting gripping essays and poetry is exceptional. Publishing ecological education pieces in mainstream education journals is thus another potentially powerful and under-utilized/under-available avenue for social change that David suggests. Many critical environmental education scholars are not taken seriously and given publishing access in wider-access education journals, and/or (subsequently) submit their work solely within the environmental education field. David suggests, "I really think that people in environmental ed that have this broad analysis of culture and environment really ought to [be able to] reach a wider audience, [and this is one place to] be more strategic about how to make an impact on the field."

Another silence follows these thoughts. Squinting at the brightness of the sky, David points North, "More redtails in that little slice of sky." We hear their cries as they prey upon the abundant rodents in the fields below. Our final interview is circling to a close. David repeats my last question, "…it's what a lot of us at these EE conferences have been talking about: what should we do as a group, how do we make a difference, how do we interrupt the status quo, how do we make an intervention? … What should be our act of civil disobedience or our intervention at this point in time? I think that's a really good question…" And this time, the question is left as a point of reflection for the future.

"How are you feeling?" I ask.

"I'm on top of the rocks! I'm feeling pretty good … I talked with Jill about how being on this end of qualitative research is interesting because you realize how inadequate a certain snapshot of text is to capture the life, you know. So. But you trust that another human being can appreciate the complexity underneath the linearity of speech acts. Snapshots of speech acts."

I acknowledge to David the brevity and limited nature of this research. "What I keep coming back to," I say, "is the idea of sharing and telling stories. Feeling that that's all I can hope for in this process."

He nods, "I hope you take away the story of my love for this land and my sadness of leaving it and my excitement about meeting another land, developing that love affair again of another place that I know I love already, or else I wouldn't be moving there." David stretches his back side to side with arms raised and calls out, "We're on top of the world, here! Can you peek through there and just see how on and on it goes?"

Transitioning

Within the time that elapsed between when I visited David and his family in Palouse (2010) and the actual writing of this portrait (2012), they moved and settled into Thunder Bay, Ontario, and David into his position at Lakehead University. The move marked a period of significant transformation. But before he left, David tells me that with "this current re-invention of myself," another one of his commitments was to engage more with what he calls "inner work" and well-being. Given David's Thoreauvian emphasis on the "whole self," this vision makes conceptual sense, but is riddled with hurdles. "If sustainability is a serious discourse and is growing in higher ed, sustainability of the people that work in higher ed isn't on the map, which isn't surprising." Part of this neglect comes from environmental education's attempts to "legitimate itself in the broader academic community," and when it comes to legitimacy, such things as well-being are considered "fluffy." I ask David whether he feels there will be more space for him to push back against that, given that his Lakehead University position is one of leadership. "Does [the CRC role] enable you to take more risks or does it pressure you to conform more?" Initially, he laughs and responds, "This is the question that keeps me up at night! This is a big struggle for me." But, eventually, David asserts that, despite fears of being marginalized or silenced, his intention is to bring more language of well-being into, for example, committee meetings. "If I want to re-invent myself and bring more of myself to the work, the institution—and I do—then I must step in this direction. … I know that academics are pretty resistant and I don't really have a lot of skill and experience … [but,] it's a good opportunity for me."

I take the three-minute walk up to Greenwood Cemetery again on my last night in town. Looking around, one can see so many stories here—not just of the people that have lived and died in Palouse, but of David's family too. The kids play hide-and-seek here, their close friend and neighbor, Marge's land borders the Western edge, and the (Greenwood) cemetery features as the letter "G" in their homemade "P is for Place" alphabet book.

Watching the sun descend over a distant horizon, I don't have to "wait for the signs" of transition. They are here. It is autumn, the light is fading on my final day in Palouse, David's family has three weeks left before they move, and as I gaze toward the radiant reds above the plains, a distant jet glints in the sunlight, heading to some far-off destination. Snapping a few photos, I try to imagine the simultaneous excitement and sadness David's family is facing. Ultimately curious as to what new beginnings this ending will bring, what new paradoxes will arise for them and which will follow them, I finally shift my focus back to the country road that will take me to my own next destination. I walk down the hill, listening again to the crunch of gravel as I place one foot in front of the other.

***

Dialogue on Integrity and Complicity

Many aspects of my time with David during the portraiture writing have remained with me. More and more, I have come to appreciate the notion of struggle and paradox as places for generative movement when I find myself questioning how to engage with my complicity. And the question about the "civil disobedience of a place-based academic" is one that has inspired the arc of my current and future research projects. When I returned to David several years later for a dialogue about this portrait, we spent much of our conversation focusing on the notion of the "inner" and "outer" self. This was something that he had discussed during our time together when I wrote the portrait. However, it was a topic that did not make it solidly into the portrait. Given that much of David's work in the time between my visit and the writing of this book has focused on inner/outer work, I am glad that we were able to come back to it…

NORA: *I went back to your portrait and want to talk with you about some of the core concepts that we explored and see what's right, what's not, and what's changed, or what we could add. If we start with the ideas of complicity or contradiction, I remember you discussing the Faustian Bargain, and we went to the gravestone… What do you think about those ideas now?*

DAVID: I haven't read that in years now, so I don't remember completely. I read your questions for our conversation today, of course. But, the idea of contradiction and complicity—sure, they're endemic to my experience of the work. If I had the choice, I wouldn't work. I mean, I would not work for money in the same way that I do.

Yes, I have an incredibly good job, to be a professor at a university and have the traditional markers of good wages and good benefits, which are so incredibly rare these days, becoming ever more rare. I have these things, and on some level, there's nothing to complain about, so why would I even talk about complicity and contradiction? You know, I got a good job! And, my responsibility within that is to make the best of it in the sense that I want to be a force for good in the world and in the institution that I work in.

But, obviously, if you step back as an intellectual and do an analysis of the universities and their role in reproducing unsustainable cultures, you recognize how bureaucratic, corporate-minded, competitive, and therefore in many ways damaging, these institutions are. And we internalize their norms. There's a lot to be worried about there. There's a lot that doesn't feel very good because feeling good and being well is not the institution's goal. There's a lot that goes unsaid, unacknowledged, a lot of institutional violence. A ton of privilege and racism—of all kinds—that really no one is immune to in these large organizations that are all hierarchically organized. So, there's a lot there that is a mirror image of the larger problems in our violent, global culture that are tough to sit with and realize that we're a part of.

So yes, I feel complicit in an institutional culture, but mainly that's not the dominant feeling. The dominant feeling now is this sense that I have a responsibility to contribute positively to that culture. And what that means, is to try to transform it, find ways to create arrangements that will benefit people and place. In other words, I think my responsibility is to figure out a way to use my position to contribute to the well-being of others who share this institution as well as the larger networks and communities that I'm a part of outside of it. But I have to start with myself.

NORA: So, you're talking a lot about responsibility. How does responsibility relate to this overriding concept of integrity that I've been interested in for this project? When I went into this project, I thought, "Well, if integrity is about 'walking the talk' or something like that, and we find ourselves unable to fully do that because we have these compromising conditions that we live within,' I think we need to have another concept of integrity." When I first visited you, I learned a lot from the way you spoke about paradox. You said that paradox was a generative site of struggle, that your greatest moments emerged from struggle. So, I'm curious whether the notion of paradox still resonates with you, when you think of integrity, and how responsibility adds in to that equation.

DAVID: Oh yes it still resonates. I don't know if I said this last time, but, I'm reminded of the fact that we're all full of contradictions. We're not like computer programs where you can push a button and it follows a logical sequence. We're not like that. We have lots of different competing needs and desires and different ways of responding to different situations and different people, depending on what's happening at that time. Things are in flux. Like Walt Whitman (1892) says, "Do I contradict myself? Very well then, I contradict myself, I am large, I contain multitudes" (section 51). That's not a cop-out from the idea of integrity. It's just a recognition that life isn't something that we play out according to our values. Our values, rather, are shaped by our interaction with life. And so, I feel like the idea of integrity is to really pay attention to my responses to tension, to the immediate environment of my experience being in the world. So, with work, it's like, "What's here for me now? What energies are calling me and trying to come forward? What needs to happen here and what is my role in it?"

There is a lot of positive creative energy in such questions. Along with what pulls me forward, I also want to recognize the fact of suffering and struggle—in everyone's life. And, as we talked about before, I think struggle can be really productive—in a good sense—productive places of maybe growth and transformation. There's just so much suffering in the world, and that reality is kind of the baseline that we enter into this work to meet. And it's like, "Okay. What's my work, my place in the world that I have?"

So, the question isn't "Am I happy right now?" Maybe it's more like, "Am I doing the right thing with my life? Is how I am holding my energies in the world, the relationships that I'm a part of, the projects that I am investing and committing time to, all the commitments that I'm making, are those right for me? Do those feel right for me?" I'm sensitive to this because I see how easy it is in higher ed to get pulled in so many different directions. There's not a professor that I know who hasn't told me that they're crazy busy, they're doing too many things, they're not doing any of it well, and it's a frustration, but they can't figure out what to do about it. This craziness is endemic to this work because of all the reward structures and cultural norms that swirl around it. And because of the autonomy which leads to so much possibility in what one might do. Am I doing the right thing among so many choices? Whitman's (1892) "I am large, I contain multitudes" (section 51) can also become a recipe for feeling overwhelmed.

NORA: Yeah. I really connect with what you said about asking yourself, "How am I holding my energies and commitments that I'm making, and are those right for me?" In your description, David, I'm also hearing you talk about how integrity has a context to it—it's very much about the present moment, the relationships and the people you're with. But, I also hear you describing it as something that's fairly internal. Something interesting that I observed when I went to visit Ray for the initial portraits was that his version of integrity seemed to be external to him, it was more about a project or shared goal that he had with First Alaskan communities. So, I'm wondering whether and how relationships with other people figure into your notion of integrity as something that unifies the different parts of the self.

DAVID: Yeah, big question, Nora. Big question. You don't mess around. I mean… okay. Hm. Well, you've started to draw a distinction between what I call inner and outer work. And what their relationship might be. And I think that it's fair to say that in Western culture—and potentially the culture of work—it's mostly all about outer work. This is very true in academe where an awareness of one's interiority is routinely demeaned as "navel gazing." Yet, in order for outer work to be work of integrity, there needs to be a harmony between one's inner work—how we really feel about our lives—and one's outer work—the public persona we bring to the workplace. How can we align our work outside with our interior work so that, as I was saying, there's some sort of a harmony there where they can be an expression of one another? I started asking these questions years ago when I first read Parker Palmer's (1998) *The Courage to Teach*. I still think that this is one of the most important, and potentially transformative, education books ever written.

In order for the inner and the outer work to align, we have to have a sense that we're doing the right thing and so we have to have a way of consciously knowing how that might feel. And part of that process for me has become checking out how it feels with my body—asking really honest questions about how I feel, and not just what I think. How do I feel is not just an intellectual question. It's intellectual, emotional, spiritual, physical—not that these are necessarily separate categories—but it's a way to describe a fuller experience of paying attention and noticing what is really happening.

There's this other great writer I was reading last year—David Whyte. He's a poet who's also written a lot about work. You might want to look at his books about work. There's this subtitle to one of his books that defines work—it's right on the cover of the book—Whyte (2002) says, "Work is the opportunity for shaping the place where the self meets the world." I really love that quote because, like you're doing, it's bringing the inner and the outer together in a way that isn't polarizing them, you know, sequestering them off into different realms. The sort of "do good" or "be productive" realm on the one hand, the "take care of myself" realm on the other. No, that's not at all what inner and outer work are about to me. Inner work and outer work are about shaping the place where the self meets the world, and that's an everyday encounter. It's also the answer to the question, what am I going do with the rest of my life?

NORA: *The question becomes—well, how do you know you're aligning inner and outer work? You said that there is this process of checking in with yourself, a fuller* experience of noticing. Personally, I find that tricky. You know, when someone asks me, "how are you?" I'm like, "Hm. Well, there's a lot of ways I could answer that question!"

DAVID: Exactly!

NORA: So, what do you look to when you seek to answer those questions now, for yourself? What cues do you use or draw upon?

DAVID: Again, it's become not so much the question of "what do I believe?" I've really become more sensitive to the important cousin to that question, which is, "How do I feel?" What signals is my body sending me and where in my body am I experiencing them? Through mindfulness practice, I've learned the power of paying attention to these signals: tightness in the abdomen or the chest, constricted breathing, contorted postures, all the ways the body holds what it is feeling. We don't think much about our emotional bodies at work, but our physical bodies sure feel it, and they often pay the price. I know mine has. This is so hard and important to talk about in academe. How do we move from merely talking ideas to communicating ways of knowing that are based on embodied emotional and spiritual experience? This has become increasingly important to me … expanding how we "think" about our work to include a wider bandwidth of ways of being and knowing that aren't just rational, intellectual discourse associated with beliefs and values. There's another level of being that is connected to my body's knowing and my intuition for what's right for me in this moment. You know, I ask myself, "What am I being called toward or pushed away from and how do I feel about it in my body?" I think, as educators interested in other ways of knowing, we need to pay much more attention to the whole human being, and not just the human thinking. This is what integrity means. To be integrated.

NORA: So, it sounds like one of the questions that you're trying to bring into your decision-making is "how does this feel for me, not only in the realm of the outer ego self, but in the realm of the inner self, and in the realm of the body as well; how does that feel, and how does that align?" You're intentionally bringing that in because it's often, as you say, marginalized and excluded as a way of justifying or thinking about our decisions.

DAVID: Yeah, and it's always present because our whole selves are always present, so which part of ourselves are we feeding and noticing? And, I would say we're feeding the egocentric parts of ourselves most of the time when we're not attuned to these other parts of being alive that aren't about bolstering the ego and the outward focused person. So, it's the *practice* of being more whole that

I'm interested in. And that's a word—whole—that requires caution because it can sound trite. But the emphasis here is on practice. I don't really know what it means to be whole—"I am large, I contain multitudes"—but I do know what it's like to feel broken and how mindfulness practice can help re-harmonize the fractured pieces.

And if you're really doing your inner work, you are practicing it beyond your meditation pillow. It follows you out into the world and it shapes all your relations. What I'm trying to get at in my own life and in this conversation is a sense of harmony between the inner and the outer so that whatever it is that I have to bring into the world, from this interior realm, finds its home in the outer realm that I'm simultaneously a part of. Inner work is not an end in itself. No, it's about integrating the parts of me in an authentic way that allows me to bring what I have out into the world in a way that serves that relationship between me and the world. That's what it's about, Nora, right? It's not about serving others, it's about having a healthy relationship between yourself and others. It's about having a relationship with others that is in service of that relationship. I'm very skeptical of people that want to serve others.

NORA: What do you mean?

DAVID: I mean that the service of others can—CAN—be an egocentric desire and it can be out of balance so easily. Serving others—*why*? You know, like, *why*? Why do *you* want to serve others? Who are *you* to serve others? It can be a missionary thing. The missionaries wanted to serve others. Well, in whose vision do you want to serve? I mean, that's a basic critical question, right? In whose interests do you want to serve others? So, the need for relationship to really frame the conversation about outward service is what I'm getting at here.

NORA: Yeah. So, it comes back to healthy relationships.

DAVID: Yeah.

NORA: In some of our conversation today and also a few years ago, we talked about the notion of privilege. And, sometimes when people hear the phrase "inner work," there is a sense that it is associated with privilege. How is privilege related to inner and outer work?

DAVID: You know, if you want to talk about privilege, I think we need to really back up and talk about privilege. I don't think that aligning one's interior world with the outer world is only for the privileged. I would in fact argue that it is "the privileged" who have made inner work almost illegal with their "privileging" of outer productivity.

NORA: Yeah, I agree, I think it's important not to make the assumption that this kind of reflective work is only available to and a product of a privileged person's life.

DAVID: I would say that assumption is historically, patently false. Look at the emergence of spirituality and religion cross-culturally around the world. Do the historical work and see how slaves responded to oppression. It's not like the oppressors simply oppressed and that's it. There's resistance and other ways of responding to oppression that allow us to be human and have an interior life even in oppressive circumstances.

Privileges don't necessarily entail doing what I call the "real work," what lots of people call the "real work," which is this balancing of the whole self, the interior, the outer. Socioeconomic privileges might sometimes enable those things, but I think they just as often reinforce egocentric modes of accumulating outer success. The existence of privilege probably more often works to accumulate outer success because that's what privilege is already entangled in, outer success.

NORA: Yeah. That makes sense. … Wow. I'm looking forward to sitting with and reflecting on all these things we've been talking about.

DAVID: Yeah. How're you doing?

NORA: This is so valuable to me, David. I am really, really grateful for you being open and vulnerable and willing to talk about these complex ideas. It's really a gift and I don't take any of it lightly. Yeah, it's…

DAVID: It's a gift to me too to just have a conversation that's real about the work that we share. It's a *rare*, it's a rare privilege (smiling), right? I think that's a very interesting word. But, I'm using it really intentionally there, it's like, that's the kind of privilege I want. To be able to talk with you about this. And it's the tip of the iceberg because this is a point in time that has been co-created by us through relationship that signifies just, you know, our separate lives and what we're trying to work through. There's a lot more than what has been said that remains unsaid.

***

New Questions

David and I talked for nearly an hour and a half the day in which the conversation above took place, and not all of that conversation is included here. A monsoon was stirring up the air outside as we talked, and just as my tape recorder recorded the redtails during my last interview with David for the portrait, the interview we had for the conversation above recorded the thunder and wind of a late-summer monsoon.

One of David's phrases from this interview that spoke most directly to this book's questions about integrity and complicity came as a response to one of my particularly long questions. I had shared the history of my motivation for engaging in this research many years ago. In response, he said: "Like Walt Whitman says, 'Do I contradict myself? Yeah, I contradict myself. I am vast. I contain multitudes.' That's not a cop-out from the idea of integrity. It's just a recognition that life isn't something that we play out according to our values. Our values are shaped by our interaction with life. And so, I feel like the idea of integrity is to really pay attention to my responses to tension, to the environment, the immediate environment."

What I hear in this phrase is that integrity is about how we shape our encounters with the world. Encounters, meetings, moments. Integrity is not about doing x, y, or z, but rather about the shaping of relationships. How do I take all of me—what I feel, what I know, what I want (which is all known and discovered in relationship)—and integrate it into this encounter with this place, this time, these people? Integrity is found there, particularly when we feel that we've been able to integrate the most authentic parts of our selves—the parts that we feel are "right" or "good"—into that encounter. David's quoting of Whyte's (2002) work leaves me with a fruitful question to hold: how am I "shaping the place where the self meets the world?"

Indeed, both my visit with David in 2010 and my dialogue with him years later left me with several fruitful questions. Throughout my time interacting with him, David continually avoided the traps of seeking purity and/or avoiding complicity, thus his insights offer questions for reflection that I find particularly grounding and helpful. In addition to the question above of how we are shaping the place where the self meets the world, David also reminded me to simply ask "How do I feel? And how does my body feel?" when I'm struggling with how to make ethical decisions in a situation riddled with complicity. His acceptance of struggle and paradox call on me to tune in at those difficult moments, for they are times of generativity, times to question: how am I spending my energy, how does my action align with my experience as a whole person, and what can I learn from this tension? Am I conforming to what my education institution says is "good," or am I critically questioning what "my neighbors call good" (Thoreau, 1995, p. 19), and repenting of my conformities to a system in which I don't believe? His interactions with peers and students inspire the exciting question: "how can we inspire and conspire together?" David's love of the land calls me to link integrity to place by asking: what signs from this place am I noticing? And, how can we consider integrity to be not only about our own becoming as people, but instead to be about the *relationship* between our own becoming and the becoming of the place with which we live? Can that relationship be as ripe with intrigue, rapture, creativity, and connection as a love affair?

Notes

1 As of 2022 and the publication of this book, David is now Professor of Education at Lakehead and no longer in the Canada Research Chair of Environmental Education role.
2 David changed his last name from Gruenewald to Greenwood in 2008.

References

Berry, W. (2012, April). It all turns on affection. *Jefferson Lecture in the Humanities.* Lecture conducted from The National Endowment for the Humanities, Washington, D.C. Retrieved July 27, 2013, from http://www.neh.gov/about/awards/jefferson-lecture/wendell-e-berry-lecture

Greenwood, D. A. (2010a). A critical analysis of sustainability education in schooling's bureaucracy: Barriers and small openings in teacher education. *Teacher Education Quarterly, 37*(4), 139–154.

Greenwood, D. A. (2010b). Nature, empire, and paradox in environmental education. *Canadian Journal of Environmental Education, 15*, 9–24.

Greenwood, D. A., & McKenzie, M. (2009). Context, experience and the socioecological: Inquiries into practice. *Canadian Journal of Environmental Education, 14*, 5–14.

Gruenewald, D. A. (2002). Teaching and learning with Thoreau: Honoring critique, experimentation, wholeness, and the places where we live. *Harvard Educational Review, 72*(4), 1–19.

Gruenewald, D. A. (2003a). At home with the other: Reclaiming the ecological roots of development and literacy. *The Journal of Environmental Education, 35*(1), 33–43.

Gruenewald, D. A. (2003b). Loss, escape, and longing for the sacred in poems about school. *Educational Studies, 34*(3), 279–299.

Gruenewald, D. A. (2003c). The best of both worlds: A critical pedagogy of place. *Educational Researcher, 32*(4), 3–12.

Gruenewald, D. A. (2006). Resistance, reinhabitation, and regime change. *Journal of Research in Rural Education, 21*(9), 1–7.

Gruenewald, D. A. (2008). Place-based education: Grounding culturally responsive teaching in geographical diversity. In *Place-based education in the global age: Local diversity* (pp. 137–154). Lawrence Erlbaum Associates.

Hardt, M., & Negri, A. (2000). *Empire*. Harvard University Press.

Kiessling, K. (1999). Victim of corporation greed: The mysterious tombstone in Palouse. *Bunchgrass Historian, 25*(1), 22–24.

Palmer, P. (1998). *The courage to teach: Exploring the inner landscape of a teacher's life.* Jossey-Bass.

Thoreau, H. D. (1993). *Civil disobedience and other essays.* Dover Publications, Inc.

Thoreau, H. D. (1995). *Walden; Or, life in the woods.* Dover Publications, Inc.

Whitman, W. (1892). Song of Myself, 51. *poets.org.* Retrieved 20 May, 2020, from https://www.poetryfoundation.org/poems/45477/song-of-myself-1892-version

Whitman, W. (1993). Leaves of grass: The "death-bed" edition. Random House, Inc.

Whyte, D. (2002). *Crossing the unknown sea: Work as a pilgrimage of identity.* Riverhead Books.

4

Madhu Suri Prakash

Happy Valley

Exhausted after a red-eye flight across the continent, I gaze out the window as our plane descends into the autumn-colored, rolling hills of Happy Valley, Pennsylvania.[1] A brisk walk into, through, and out of the tiny airport, followed by a welcome inhale of balmy fall air, begins to waken my senses. Although I do not see her right away, my exhaustion is replaced with excitement and anticipation as I scan the sidewalks and parking lot for my host. After only two minutes sitting in the sunny grass, I catch sight of bold reds, oranges, and blacks lightly blowing in the breeze. Laughing with affection and joy before we even make eye contact, a vivacious woman—beautiful and radiant—walks toward me with arms extended.

Full Professor at Pennsylvania State University,[2] Madhu Suri Prakash would, over the course of the next week that I spend with her, describe herself in various ways: a philosopher of education, yes. But also: a daughter, a mother, a loner, a friend, a Luddite, and, simply, soil. I came to visit Madhu because of her unique emphasis on oppressive colonial forces within the field of environmental education, her experience therein, and her animated interest in participating in this research.

Madhu had insisted on picking me up at the airport as if there would have been no other option. After our initial hug and "nice to finally meet you!" we walk toward her car as she asks how to best make me comfortable, rested, fed, and cared for. I offer mixed answers of both thanks and polite deferrals. Stopping briefly at her modest, cozy home, I discover that she has already prepared dinner for myself and her friend (at whose house I stayed), she has purchased groceries for me for the week, and she makes me breakfast as I use her phone to call home. Madhu tells me that in her culture, guests are god; if you are not the best host possible, you are not showing respect to divinity. Guests need to know that they matter. Sipping warm tea, hunched over a bowl of freshly cut fruit and yogurt, I sit at her table wearing her red silk slippers. I am utterly wrapped in hospitality. Half an hour later, Madhu drops me off to rest with my groceries, a delicious homemade dinner, and a box of Bengal spice tea that she tossed on top as we headed out the door.

Assembly Line

Looking for entrepreneurial possibilities in a remote Oaxaqueña village, a New Yorker stumbles upon the home of a basket maker. The basket maker weaves locally gathered and hand-dyed grasses into intricate and individual works of art. Living off the food of his land and largely outside of a monetary economy, he weaves on his porch when his daily work is done. The New Yorker sees opportunities for profit and returns home to work up a scheme by which the baskets could be sold as wrapping for fancy pralines at a New York sweet shop. However, when the New Yorker attempts to finalize the deal back in México, the basket weaver surprises him with his accounting. As the number of baskets he is asked to make rises, so does his price per basket. Taking into account the whole picture, the basket weaver figures in the time that he would be away from his farm, the time needed to find the right insects and plants for dyes, the time needed to properly tend the drying grasses, and the effort of weaving a bit of his soul and song into each. Ultimately baffled by the basket weaver's apparent disinterest in profit, the New Yorker and basket weaver part ways, each returning to his own distinct worldview and way of life.

This is a synopsis of the short story "Assembly Line," published in 1966 by B. Traven, a story that appears in Madhu's course reader and, indeed, in much of her conversation. She regularly uses this story as a metaphor for educational systems, where institutionalized education operates through the mass production

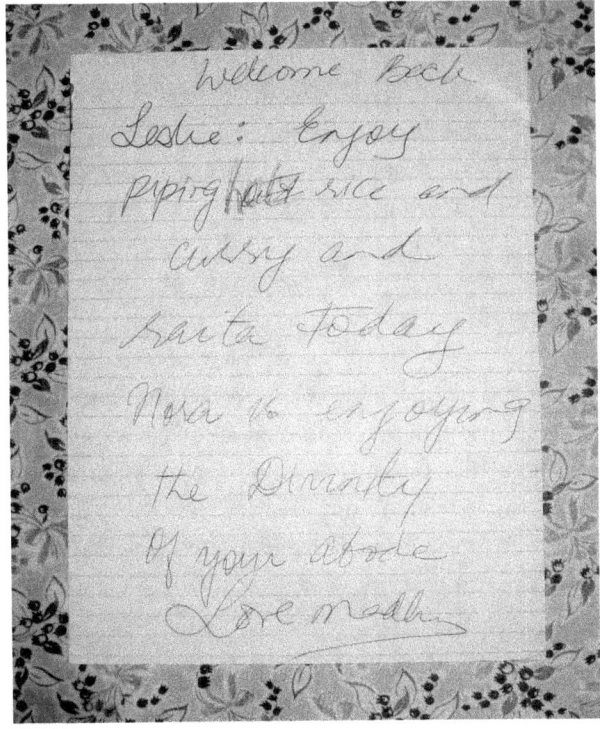

Figure 4.1. Guests Are God
A note from Madhu to her good friend Leslie, with whom I stayed while I was in town: "Leslie: Welcome back! Enjoy piping hot rice and curry and raita today. Nora is enjoying the Divinity of your abode. Love, Madhu" Source: Author.

of graduates, rubber-stamped through a gamut of courses and certifications until they are deemed suitable to join the global economy. When sharing this story, Madhu "admires the Oaxaqueña basket weaver" and bemoans the influence of the "assembly line" mentality and institution that drove the interests of the New York businessman. Her 2008 book, *Escaping Education: Living as Learning within Grassroots Cultures*, would suggest that the basket weaver from the story was lucky to have "escaped" from the "assembly line" of the global economy. In that same logic, she considers those who live and thrive within land-based economies lucky to escape the colonizing forces of modern education and "development."

Madhu's academic work traces how mainstream, modern education has become equated with "development," "boxing" people and cultures into categories of "developed" and "un/under-developed." In so doing, the traditional knowledge of land-based cultures is not only under-valued and ignored, it is looked upon as "backward and uncivilized." Institutionalized education is spreading in concert with the global economy, from one "un-developed" place to another. In its wake, it leaves behind the false promise of "better" jobs, "improved" lifestyles, and the "skills" to progress beyond subsistence living. Yet, the global economy cannot accommodate the thousands of newly educated people from "developing" nations. Led astray on a "road to nowhere" and having traded land-based skills/knowledge for global-economy skills/knowledge, graduates are frequently left jobless and estranged from their traditional land, people, and practices (Prakash & Esteva, 2008, 2011; Prakash & Stuchul, 2004).

In contrast to this type of institutional education, Madhu celebrates a living-as-learning, cultural transmission approach to teaching and learning about the world. These un-institutionalized, traditional approaches draw from a deep well of Indigenous wisdom that she calls "common sense." Common sense is about the ways in which people relate to one another and their places. It arises from a belonging to place, an intimate knowledge of that place, and a self-sustaining community that passes on that knowledge. Madhu eloquently explained to me, "Common sense is that other sixth sense that comes from belonging to a commons. The other five senses are deprived when we are in just engineered spaces. … But that sixth sense, that's called common sense, requires belonging … to a place, requires belonging to the people of that place, requires understanding how that place in turn is connected to all places, that we all in a sense live downstream."

What I find fascinating and challenging about these two very different approaches to education that Madhu's work explores is how they are intertwined in her own life. As a professor of education and teacher-educator, she is at times required to take on the role of the New York businessman, with her own role to play in the "assembly line" of education. And also, as a daughter and grandchild of land-based women, she is intimately familiar with common sense, as is the basket weaver. The interplay of these values and worldviews challenges Madhu to negotiate a situation where forces pull in sometimes opposite directions, and contradiction becomes inevitable.

The Roots of Rasa

"Rajinder's Remarkable Rasoi," an article published in *Yes! Magazine*, was the first written piece of hers that Madhu shared with me. Giving glimpses of the life and lessons of her first teacher, her mother Rajinder, this article and others divulge the cultural landscape that nurtured Madhu's sense of hospitality and relationship.

As was revealed on my first day with her, Madhu's hospitality is often centered on food—cooking, serving, eating, growing, and composting food. From her mother, she learned the simple yet sacred ways of going about these acts. She writes, "Only when food is prepared with love, with reverence and respect not only for the eater and the eaten, but for our Creator and all of Creation, do people become adept in the art of bringing out the juices—the rasa—that flows from all the vegetables, fruits and other ingredients that go into the sublime and sacred preparation of food" (Prakash, 2009, p. 49). Like the Oaxaqueña basket weaver, Madhu's understanding of food transcends both physical and spiritual sustenance; it connects families, communities, plants, animals, soil, water, and sun.

In particular, Madhu's passion for food is rooted in a larger love of soil. Talking over her round dining table, she spends most of our first interview expounding on common sense, food, water, and soil. Next to her is a stack of favorite books, and midway through our conversation, she reaches out to Wendell Berry's (1990) *What are People For?* When I tell her I haven't read it, her response is, "ecstasy awaits you." Happily sharing the many insights she has had from this book, Madhu paraphrases Berry's thoughts on the very purpose of life: "We human beings have no more important task to do than keeping our soil regenerated, our physical soil and the culture that knows how to sustain that soil in place." And, flipping through the well-worn pages of the book, she reads aloud, "These two kinds of accumulation, of local soil and local culture, are intimately related and the most important task for any people to do." The care and renewal of soil is thus etched into Madhu's sense of our very purpose for living. Madhu also recognizes soil as not only something to care for, but fundamentally as herself. She remembers several years ago, when she was collecting fallen leaves from her neighbors, the boy from across the street came over to see what she was doing. Madhu told him she was "piling them up to make soil," and then reached down, grabbing the flesh of her forearm with an emphatic shake, and added, "I love to make soil because, you know, I *am* soil. This is all going to become soil." I am soil. We are soil. Preserving oneself means preserving soil, and vice versa. It is all connected.

Figure 4.2. Madhu's Backyard Hostas

I was surprised to discover that Madhu's paper "waste" isn't recycled, but is instead piled below and between mounds of dirt, plants, and leaves in her backyard. She uses it to make soil. If her yard were carpeted with a uniformly green, trim lawn, I would have noticed stacks of paper lying around. But Madhu's yard—front and back—has as little grass in it as possible. She calls it her "no-mow" strategy. Wanting to avoid all mowing and tending of grass, she has planted as many bushes, trees, shrubs, flowers, vines, and veggies as she (or any of her friends who come to help) can manage. Any gifts of hardy houseplants likely will not be found in the house at all, but instead will be tucked into the soil, adding to the lush landscape of her backyard. Source: Author.

Most notable and distinct among Madhu's soil-making skills is her practice of "separating shit from state." Collaborating with a Mexican friend, she worked to create and utilize a "dry toilet" that "does not make human waste, it makes golden soil... it is the *best* fertilizer that otherwise people use factories to make." Madhu suggests that common sense can be represented by the separation of shit from state. "Common sense comes when people say, 'We will take care of our shit. We do not need the state to treat our shit.' We can do it by... keeping our shit in our own house instead of sending it to other people's fields, instead of sending it to the oceans ... [or] a sewage treatment plan that is managed by the state and that supports a *massive* trillion dollar chemical industry of the sort that Rachel Carson would *easily* say is the cause of silent spring."

Madhu actively articulates the connections between food, people, and soil in our conversations as well. Her words echo familiar strains in ecological philosophy... Humans are "part of the natural world ... not separate, ... not other." "We are knots in a big web of life," and "profoundly connected with the whole cosmos." But, in her mother's kitchen, where the rasa flowed daily, these connections were so omnipresent as to remain nameless. With a dual sense of both admiration and loss, Madhu explains that what her family "had in their blood, coursing from the minute they drank their mother's milk was such a sense and sensibility of knowing without having the words of the 'earth's limits'!"

Enhancing the contrast between admiration and loss, Madhu shifts her perspective out of her mother's kitchen into the here-and-now, into her role as professor, analyst of cultural colonization. She describes how the things that were important and valued to her mother, grandmother, and great-grandmother were not taught in schools, nor were they important or valued to those who were "educated." Land-based knowledge was not a part of her formal schooling. Madhu recalls, "we didn't call it education, we called it common sense. It's what commoners had. But, to become educated, we had to go beyond common sense, because [sarcastically] after all, everyone has common sense, even illiterate people." Having experienced a common sense-based education alongside a Westernized, school-based education, she says, "My *best* experiences were outside walled classrooms...taking place just being raised by mothers and grandmothers who were not educated. ... They happened so subtly that I didn't even notice them, like fish don't notice water ... it didn't belong to the classroom because no classroom ever brought it up." And further, "I feel *sooo happy* to be part of something that I was earlier taught to dismiss as *not* education. *They're right*—it is not education, it is cultural transmission of a culture of sustainability that never called it that, it just called itself Hindustani culture."

Schooling and De-Schooling

Afternoon sun slants through two narrow windows onto a horseshoe of navy blue desks. Madhu's Philosophy of Education class, a mandatory course for pre-service teachers, is meeting for the third time during my week in town. Madhu had requested that I come for this particular week because of the relationships and trust that she felt would be established between her and the students by this, the halfway point through the semester. Today, she exhibits this trust by sharing some of her own story. Although she is happy now about her roots in common sense, she did not always feel this way. Assuring the class that she is on "a journey

... [and] nothing I say is final," she asks us to open her and Gustavo Esteva's (2008) *Escaping Education* to page 88. She reads aloud:

> On January 20, 1949, President Truman took office and launched a new era for global development: "We must embark on a bold new program for making the benefits of our scientific advances and industrial progress available for the improvement and growth of underdeveloped areas. The old imperialism—exploitation for foreign profit—has no place in our plans. What we envisage is a program of development based on the concepts of democratic fair dealing (Truman 1949, 114–115)."
>
> ... On January 20, 1949, two billion people became underdeveloped. In a very real sense, they ceased being what and who they were... the heterogeneous and diverse social majorities reduced to the homogenizing and narrow terms of the social minorities. (p. 88–89)

A dramatic pause follows her reading. "I'd like you to think of a time when you have been boxed. When you were judged or labeled by someone else," Madhu says. Slowly at first, students raise their hands to share stories. Soon, there are more hands up than can be answered. Students share personal memories of their own marginalization, or in some cases, how they have marginalized others. Afterward, Madhu shares her own.

Growing up in military schools, Madhu was considered privileged to have access to a quality Western education, a "modern" education that considered "everything that my people represented [as] backwardness and underdevelopment." Reflecting her own experiences of being "boxed" and "boxing" others, she describes her childhood distaste for her black hair and envy of Barbie's blond locks. Thus carrying the weight of the cultural colonization of India, Madhu walks us through her past as she "progressed" through her bachelor's, two master's degrees, and eventually a PhD from Syracuse University. Between her master's and PhD, she moved to the United States and shifted disciplines from economics to education. Her goal was to learn all she could about "this [again, sarcastic:] '*fabulous*' democracy of America and take it back to transform India."

During her first year as a professor at Penn State, Madhu's adopted father, a respected professor himself, brought in a scholar to give a lecture series. Although she had not before heard of this scholar, she quickly learned that he was regarded as an audacious theorist that was allegedly "anti-feminist and anti-gender equality," and that he would supposedly "squash you like a fly with a fly squasher" if you asked him any questions. Skeptical, yet curious, Madhu attended. At the end of his first lecture, she marched down to personally ask him, "Are you against

Figure 4.3. Arranging the Classroom
Each day, Madhu has her students re-arrange the typical rows of desks (shown above) to form a semi-circle so they can see one another. During my visits, however, even though students face each other, they remain deferential to her, raising their hands to be called upon, and Madhu's voice presides over the conversation. Source: Author.

gender equality?" After one glance at her, his sharp response was, "I do not wish to speak with you." This was Madhu's first introduction to Ivan Illich.

In the years following, Illich gave many more lectures at Penn State, eventually becoming a visiting scholar from 1986–1998. Madhu initially regarded him with contempt. "I started teaching *Deschooling Society*[3] more to teach his foolishness, but the more I taught it to ridicule it, the more it taught me, and the more it forced me to stand my ideas about education on my head." She learned with time that Illich critiqued liberal, feminist notions of gender equality that were predicated upon capitalism and essentially espoused equal opportunity for exploitation, favoring instead a culturally based, vernacular understanding that was anti-capitalist and anti-colonial. After a 5-year transition from contempt to admiration, she made her peace with him: "I went to his home, ate humble pie, shared his pasta." Ivan Illich became an incredible influence in Madhu's life, both in State College and outside. Illich split "each academic year between guest professorships at Penn State and in Bremen, Germany, and [spent] the remaining months in a Mexican village outside Cuernavaca working on various writing projects" (Snell, 1995, p. 1). Madhu recalls that when he was in town, "all of his seminars involved cooking fresh, local food at home," and that his home was a gathering place for local and international radical thinkers and activists.

As Madhu began accepting Illich's ideas, she also encountered Wendell Berry (e.g. 1987; 1990) and David Orr (e.g. 1992; 2004), further contributing to a radical shift in her philosophy of education. "Just when I thought I knew philosophy of education, everything I knew was being called into question by these people. It was very liberating; it was very shattering. I had to lift myself out of the debris of all my ideas being smashed." She learned about the "abject immorality of the 'development' enterprise" and how "development" and the education system go hand in hand. It was alongside this critique when Madhu began to recognize that her "best, best, best forms of cultural initiation were taking place just being raised by mothers and grandmothers who were not educated … just being alive and living as education." She tells us, "It was Wendell Berry who first gave me the idea of contrasting the cultures of 'development' and juxtapose them to soil cultures," and it was Berry and Illich who helped her to re-discover Gandhi as well. For these lessons, Madhu freely expresses "a lot of gratitude to Orr, Illich, Berry. They have transformed my philosophy of education completely. And they've brought me back to my mothers and grandmothers by showing the centrality of where we can start with ecological literacy."

Rapt with attention to her dramatic pauses and passionately inflected voice, the students cannot help nodding in agreement as Madhu transitions from her story back to the quotes from her book. "My hope is that you will never, ever use the words 'under- over- developed' or 'developing' unless you use them in scare quotes because they are *foul* words. Just as those same words that you described others calling you in your stories of being boxed." And so, seeing as how she had just drawn a strong connection between education and "development," Madhu asks her future K-12 teachers, "What's keeping me here?" Considering the basket weaver lucky to have escaped education, why would she be part of a College of Education, part of the "assembly line," helping to train future teachers? She immediately offers one answer, "We have to, in some ways, stay slave to the system to share within it the insights we had [in] class [today]." As she says these words, my pencil races to keep up with them and I make a note to follow up during our next interview.

Later, Madhu finishes class with an acknowledgment of her students' participation, "thank you for sharing," and with some advice for their next assignment: "It should be great fun. If you're not having fun writing that essay, you'll be punished!" She laughs, and over the end-of-class rustling and sliding of desks back into standard rows, I hear snippets of comments from students to Madhu… "You've completely changed my view of what a teacher should be… my job is almost harder now, but I'm more invested…" "This class has taught me everything about how…" "…coming out of the darkness of it…" "We, being in this classroom, we have a choice to be involved in standard school or not…" "You are different than any other teacher I've ever had and that's so refreshing." And finally, once most students have left the room, a group of three are left talking in the corner about where they can buy organic onions for their group assignment due in Madhu's class next week.

Post-Shattering: Re-Arranging the Pieces

Before Madhu and I make space to talk about the story and insights she shared with her class, I visit the home of one of Madhu's former graduate students, now her good friend and colleague, Dana Stuchul. Gusty fall winds blow thousands of leaves across our view of her backyard garden and cobb oven. Warming myself with blueberry tea, I wrap my hands around the hot mug and listen to Dana's stories. Madhu and Dana initially met at Illich's Penn State lectures. Madhu would sometimes bring her 6-year-old son with her, softly speaking to him in Hindi, lovingly stroking his hair. Dana says that she first noticed Madhu because she fell in love with the relationship Madhu had with her son. That, and the fact that Madhu was the only one in the Penn State College of Education who she could turn to if she wanted to study Illich. (Madhu later told me, "no one had *ever, ever* come to see me especially interested in Ivan Illich. I couldn't believe my luck. This totally committed, brilliant, wonderful, hard-working, creative woman … because she had heard—not just from our campus but from others as well—that Madhu is the only one who takes Illich seriously.")

From her unique perspective as student, colleague, and friend, Dana was witness to some of the "post-shattering" Madhu experienced in the years after her beliefs about education underwent dramatic changes. Dana remembers when Madhu attempted to reconcile her new philosophy with her "hard-won" "developed person's life," leaving State College to travel to India "on a quest to [re-]root herself and her son in a community or village with eco-sensibilities." Madhu was engaged in this search for 2.5 years of Dana's PhD program, and Dana reminisces on how difficult it was to communicate remotely with Madhu, only over computer (in the early 2000s). Madhu was also traveling to México during those

2.5 years as she completed two book projects that pushed her toward promotion as full professor. Wanting to leave in search of something more fully outside of the "assembly line," Dana says that Madhu's promotion represented a kind of institutional welcome and acceptance that, even while she worked hard and felt satisfaction for it, she also wanted to resist. Eventually, in the face of many challenges, Madhu put her quest to permanently relocate to rest, falling instead into an annual migration between three places (strikingly similar to that of Illich) where each winter Madhu visits family in India for 1–2 months, and each summer she spends 2–3 months in her second, chosen home of Cuernavaca, México. At this point, Madhu has deep gratitude for State College as her home base, as the home where she has stability and support through many loving friends and neighbors, chief among whom is Dana.

In addition to recounting the personal transformation Madhu went through as a result of her shift in philosophy, Dana also witnessed changes in Madhu's approach to work. She describes how, "In the last decade, Madhu has taken a giant step back from the university." Whereas Madhu was the head of her department's program in Education Theory and Policy when Dana was in school, Madhu is much less involved in typical academic service these days. She is more interested in student-led, action-oriented groups, feeling that some of her previous service work was useless. Similarly, Dana notes that, "Madhu is not taking on many grad students anymore … but if she finds someone and falls in love, the formula changes." She wonders if Madhu's disinterest is because graduate students are more set in their views and less open to exploring the transformative potential of Illich and Berry's thought than undergraduates. Regardless of the reason, it is clear that Dana is one of those students who—years ago—Madhu fell in love with. And to this day, as colleagues and collaborators, Dana and Madhu share a deep, close friendship.

With my notebook enriched with Dana's memories and impressions, I walk the six blocks from her house to Madhu's. The wild wind flies down the street and the autumn deciduous trees are brilliant against a gray sky, and I reflect on the many conversations I am having with Madhu's students on my visit. Madhu arranges eight total interviews for me with her current and past students. At most of the interviews, she brings me to her favorite local food café/farmers' market, introduces me to her students, then says something like, "tell Nora about the time when…" or "tell Nora about your experience in my class when you…" or "tell Nora about how you transformed from not caring to caring…" before hurrying off to a meeting and leaving us alone to talk.

Madhu's other current and former students emphasize how her philosophy of education takes shape in a mutual sharing of personal, experiential learning. They explain how, for each journal entry her students write, they are asked to identify one new action they will take in their life starting *tomorrow* as a result of what they are learning. "She would challenge her students with committing to changes in their lives that must happen *now*, not later, not tomorrow, right *now*," says one former student. Another remembers how Madhu "talks about the shit in the world, but always with examples of solutions, hope." He quotes Berger (1984, p. 18): "The naming of the intolerable is itself a hope." Overall, Madhu's former students that I spoke to all agree that her pedagogical approach solicits transformation, and while the content of her courses explicitly focuses on ecology and education, the underlying issues at hand are the personal growth and philosophy of her students. "The deeper goals are for students to explore their selves as human beings… to find their own moral action, in which lies happiness and joy in doing what they think is right," says another student.

With the expectation or hope for transformation that she has, Madhu's students describe how their relationship with her blurs the lines between personal and professional. "Having a relationship with Madhu as a teacher is like friendship. She asks favors of you and she gives back. There's respect, you are treated equally." Another student reveals, "Madhu is like my mom, she trusts me and I can share with her." Peter Buckland, a current PhD student of hers with whom I spend an afternoon walking through State College and a nearby forest, explains how "to be Madhu's student is to be in relationship, to meet her halfway." As we weave our way through the twisting trails and out toward the edge of a field full with rustling corn stalks, Peter contemplates his relationship with Madhu. Perhaps inspired by the rich smells and sounds, the warm sun gracing us as we sit and rest, Peter comes up with the word "carnal." He says that Madhu does not ignore or separate "food, shit, sex, bodies, flowers, hugs, kisses…" If you have a relationship with her, you can expect that she will embrace and talk about the embodied aspects of being human.

When I follow up with Madhu on the stories Dana, Peter, and other students shared with me, Madhu confirms their insights into how she has re-arranged her teaching and academic commitments to—as much as possible—reflect the education she has now come to value. Regarding departmental politics, Madhu confirms Dana's sense that she took a giant step back from typical academic engagement: "While the polar bears are dying, we're worried about… how many committees we can sit on, we're sitting on 20 committees. … How can [my service] be less about me and my ego and my curriculum vitae and more about the beauty of the earth, the beauty of the people?" Similarly, Madhu asserts, "I'm really not interested in churning out a lot of doctorates, at all." Part of this disinterest stems from her dislike of her department's internal politics that emerge when assigning PhD students upon admission to faculty members. However, a second, deeper part of her disinterest in supervising many PhD students arises from her sense that both she and her department are incompatible with many graduate students' needs. Departmentally, she explains, students who are interested in environmental and ecological education are required to take years of courses that Madhu sees as largely "irrelevant" to them, as ecological and environmental issues are more-or-less ignored in her department. Furthermore, Madhu finds that when she works with graduate students who want to embark on a typical academic career, the relationship is often not fulfilling for either of them, as Madhu does not believe in typical academic work. "I think for their future, for what they're really seeking, the kind of jobs, etcetera, they're better off with other mentors… given the kind of careers they want."

Madhu also confirms her students' observations of her classroom teaching. In contrast to the educational philosophy she taught prior to engaging with Illich, Berry, Orr, and Gandhi, Madhu now centers her courses on food and ecology, actually and metaphorically. I myself observed her beginning her Thursday class by telling the students, "This course is about food for the mind, belly, and human spirit." And later, talking one on one, she explains to me, "I'm most compelled by food. It's something we have such an intimate relationship with, and it's something we can make changes on here, today." Her writing echoes this centrality: "I am slowly learning to reconnect food and waste (instead of schizophrenically severing their relationship) as the center of my courses in philosophy of education" (Prakash, 2011, p. 48). She says, "Good food is essential to a good life."

Other adaptations, however, have proved more difficult. When I ask her if she takes her classes outside, she shakes her head and explains how difficult it is because of the distracting noise, students' allergies, and weather. Madhu also recalls how, for 5 years, she attempted to start a garden at Penn State and other local schools but encountered either too much resistance or not enough interest. "My journey has been to see every school on earth have a garden. All my [gardening] attempts at different schools have really amounted to nothing."

Most recently, Madhu has found opportunities outside of Penn State for a fuller professional reconciliation of her philosophy with her teaching. In 2009, Vandana Shiva asked Madhu to assist with a course that she, Satish Kumar, and Samdhong Rimpoche had been teaching on "Gandhi and Globalization" at the University of the Seed in India. The learning in this course and others at the

University of the Seed is enriched by teachers whose "lives teach as much as the words and stories they share," and by non-credentialized Elders who are brought in to teach credentialed courses. Madhu thrives here, a place where the "knowledge and wisdom of soil, of seed, of eating, cooking, nourishing soil, etcetera," is sought after and passed on. Harkening back to her own roots, she is able to utilize her academic work within a setting that celebrates "cultural transmission" and values the knowledge of her own mother and grandmothers.

Awareness in/of the Assembly Line

As my last night in State College winds down, our bellies are full of tomato ginger soup, avocado, fresh mozzarella, brown rice, and shrikhand—a magical combination of yogurt, cardamom and saffron. Long after the sun has set, Madhu and I are nestled on opposite ends of her couch and I have the chance to ask her about her statement that we sometimes have to stay slave to the system to bring awareness into it, to show, as she says, "the absolute, abject immorality of the development enterprise and [how] development really requires the educational system, they go hand in hand." And beyond this, to "celebrate what [common people] have, honor what they have, and stop comparing them as lesser than us."

I often assume that, at least to a certain degree, complicity and contradiction are an inevitable part of life. But as she explains her ideas, Madhu's words re-frame this assumption. Referring to Illich, she describes contradiction as one of the hardships of the "modern, easy life." We have cars, planes, trains, TV, fast food, all of these so-called luxuries, but one of the heaviest burdens that comes with them (for her at least) is contradiction.

"The kinds of freedoms and autonomy we want in order to live sustainably, in order to live with ecological literacy, are destroyed by the very institutions within which we are all living. *That's* the contradiction."

"And you live with that contradiction to give awareness to your students?" I ask.

"Mm-hm. And that's plenty. ... As I look open-eyed and humbly at my own contradictions, maybe I take solace in the fact that, till he drew his last breath, Ivan Illich basically taught in universities." Madhu likewise notes that another of her "heroes," Wendell Berry, although he resigned from academic work based on a recognition of the same type of contradiction she speaks of, did come back several times, also drawn toward teaching. And yet, despite her positioning of Illich and Berry as mentors, Madhu recognizes that their projects were/are different than her own: "Both Illich and Berry are no longer interested in trying to do, for example, what all of us are seeking to do within the educational system, which is making it more humane, to make it more ecological, to make it more sustainable. I, for one, have spent my life seeing how my own classrooms can be kinder places, gentler places, more affirming places, more moral places. Where people get a taste and savor some notions of human generosity and kindness from one another, that's what I seek to cultivate. It's not that Berry or Illich dismiss these efforts, it's just not what interests them."

Still referring to Berry, Madhu adds, "I truly cannot even imagine anybody in the United States living more rooted, living more sustainably. ... He's very open and honest about his contradictions. If he can look at all those contradictions, and not exactly make his peace, but recognize that he's not going to make them disappear... then, imagine me in suburbia. ... I'm still miles away from alleviating contradictions, I'm still living a very developed person's life.

"I'm a professor of education. I'm in a College of Education. And I'm seeing all the counter-productivity of the educational enterprise and then talking about it, and then living with that talk. ... Yes, I *live* in *continual* contradiction. And there are days when it feels like an enormous burden. And other days where I'm light and see that as the human predicament. And, you know, *stop* blaming anybody, including myself ... and just make peace with *all* my own limitations and the limitations of the context within which I work, reflect and teach. And it's *okay* on those days; I wear the contradiction lightly. And there are other days of sorrow where I wear it very heavily. Doesn't do anyone any good, but it comes with the territory. ... People want some handy solution to fix the contradiction, and there isn't one. ... At some juncture, I guess, one can continue to be very sad about it all, or make some kind of peace."

Madhu continues, "Ivan Illich says, 'we all have to carry our own cross. To be human is to have the cross,' (if one is speaking of the human condition in Christian terminology). And so, it doesn't matter where you look, each person has their own brand, their own type of cross."

"Even the basket weaver?" I ask.

"Yes, of course," Madhu responds. "He's not living in utopia or paradise, he's living in reality, ... the reality of *millions* of peasants. In addition to the fact that he spends many, many hours growing his food on the soil, [he faces] all the challenges of being surrounded by developers. [Even though] he finds his own capacity to make beauty, to create beauty, to do good work... he has his crosses."

I ask for clarification, "Is the cross a hard life, or is the cross contradiction? Or is [the cross] the hard life that can take shape as contradiction?"

"Yes, yes," she confirms, it is the latter. "The hard life in my life takes the form of contradictions. His cross is of a different kind. And, I don't want his cross, but neither do I want to hand him mine thinking it's lighter. … I can't ever present my privileges as a reason for anyone else to envy me in the world. … When I go to villages in India, I really do not come away thinking, 'I have an enviable life.' I just see enough beauty, enough humanity in other people's existence to not want those juxtapositions and comparisons with my own. … Needless to say, there are thousands of people suffering in war zones, women and men beaten to earn enough money to make a few tortillas. I recognize the nature of other people's crosses. But, saying all that, and being grateful for the fact that I'm not beholden to a husband, a brutal husband, or … for a landlord oppressing me because I'm on a rented field or a rented apartment for that matter. I recognize there are all those forms of crosses… and that mine, I know how to carry it, somewhat. Somewhat. [I'm] experiencing many joys on a daily basis."

We are both silent for a moment. As I process our conversation, my eyes leisurely look over the colorful artwork that fills Madhu's walls. We both turn to watch a small, gray, ancient-looking bug as it slowly marches down her arm. She laughs quietly and we remark how these little creatures have been crawling up and down the curtain behind us and on and off Madhu for the last half hour. With affection, she tells me that they're everywhere. "I don't even know their name," she chuckles. I am reminded of how she described her mother's knowledge… "a sense and sensibility of knowing without having the words of the 'earth's limits.'" How like Madhu, I think… to love and know something without knowing or needing to know its name.

***

Dialogue on Integrity and Complicity

Among my many hopes for this book is that readers appreciate the beauty and wisdom of the people that are the subjects of these portraits and stories. With Madhu, it felt as if I could not help but convey this. Her insight shone through no matter how well I succeeded at analyzing and storytelling. Even years later, I will sometimes tear up when I go back and read this portrait of Madhu. There is something about the combination of joy, kindness, authenticity, and enthusiasm within her demeanor that is piercing. When Madhu and I engaged in a dialogue to follow up on this portrait years later, I started the conversation picking up on the thread of the "cross to bear" that we had ended with all those years ago. This particular notion was important for me because it showed a different conception of contradiction, one that did not assume that it was inevitable for everyone. I wanted to learn more about this notion, but soon after our dialogue began, Madhu shared something else. She had newer and different things to add…

NORA: When we met for my original research, we had a wonderful conversation about contradiction as one type of "cross to bear" that comes with the "modern" life. You eloquently explained how everyone has different types of crosses, and you wouldn't want to judge which ones are better or worse, but that contradiction is one type of "cross" that comes with a modern, industrial life. Do these ideas still have resonance for you in terms of how you think about complicity and integrity in your life?

MADHU: Yes, of course. And of course, in 6 years, so many things happen that other things fade into a backdrop, something else comes to the forefront. My notions of integrity have evolved in light of some very important experiences.

Last semester I was teaching two courses. In the grad seminar on contemporary philosophies of education, I told students that it would be writing intensive—three pages a week—but one page a week can be poetry, something, but it is a page about them that gives me insight about their love, passions, what matters to them. The first time they wrote, they were very enthusiastic, but by week two, some simply chose not to do it. They found it too much work.

The only person doing it was a Mexicana, doing two degrees, extremely pregnant—belly is as big as her height, she's undocumented, lived in US since age of 5, is now 25 or 26 years old. Summa cum laude in mathematics from Texas A&M. Mother died of cancer 4 years ago, oldest of seven siblings, father is jailed. None of her other siblings wanted the 6-, 9-, and 10-year-olds. In a high-risk pregnancy, so high-risk that she has to take a 2–3-hour bus ride to the next biggest town for appointments. Chances of her and baby dying are high. Outside their front door is the main highway, so they can't let the kids out to play. And every morning they have to pick up their beds so they can open up the door. She's the opposite of a needy person.

Hardest working responsible student I've seen. Papers in on time. I'm blown away by this woman, humbled by her, and I've fallen totally in love with her. Her courage. I asked her, "How can I be of some use to you? Do you need pots and pans? Cooking, food??" She said, "No, but because I'm so pregnant that I can't get down to ground to eat, I need a dining table and chairs."

I was really having a difficult semester in many, many, many fronts. I was exhausted and sleeping badly because of other anxieties. Helping her—the table was only the beginning—opened me up to my community because I couldn't help her alone. I went to all these places, I talked to so many people, and they got involved. And somehow, being able to give hundreds of hours to this family, and being able to bring basic things, and seeing the goodness, say, in a church—in the poorest church in our region, and *how* they give, they weren't at all concerned that I wasn't a Christian, they didn't care that she was undocumented, they just saw that she didn't have even one diaper for her kid, not one onesie. But somehow, anytime I was doing something—*anything*, and seeing these kids' faces light up, I don't know. It was so regenerative.

I realized that when I'm engaged with people in this kind of way, my own narcissism starts to erode and I feel better. This whole engagement has turned out to be the most joyful engagement I have done in the whole year. My life has changed.

The amount my joy has multiplied in being part of this network of joy… I feel I would be such a lesser being had I not had this in my life. I feel so blessed. So blessed in their presence. I have this feeling, "wow, I am good because I am part of something good."

But, I'm talking about this student to juxtapose her with others who I find draining, and to illustrate my understanding of integrity. I'm going to bring up another Illich (1988) piece; it's an essay written many years ago, *The Educational Enterprise in the Light of the Gospel*. In it, Illich speaks about these so-called "good teachers" as having their "Schindler's list:" they know they can't save everyone, so they're going to focus their energies on a few. I've been thinking about this Schindler's list idea. Invariably in class, there are people who give a lot of energy and then you find yourselves not depleted by them, and so you give them a lot of energy. But then there are the depletors. There are students who I have felt like every minute, every hour I would invest in them was zero return. Like, *zero*.

So, I had to ask myself: am I making my Schindler's list, or am I doing something *quite* different? Was I being a Schindler [by tending so fiercely to my amazing connection with my Mexicana student]? Perhaps. But the trouble was she was *so good*. And so courageous and so strong. That she required the least of me. There were others I had to meet after class just to *get them to start working*. Depression, students who couldn't get medical attention, needed extensions, [there were all kinds of reasons why some did not engage.]

Out of all of this, Dana [Stuchul] and I started to articulate my whole philosophy of education—it's Dana's genius actually—she said it: "genius is as common as dirt." Do we have the love, the integrity, to seek out different people's genius? And I *really tried. I really tried* with the students who weren't engaging. Because it's my third last semester. And for me, it became summarized as: how can I spread my capacity for joy?

For example, in my undergrad class, there was a student who couldn't get medical attention—one of the best students. She dropped, but came back to tell everyone she was dropping out. When she did, they all came out of the closet with tears of joy because they found they weren't alone. Everyone has a sad story to tell.

Our integrity now demands of us that we start with the premise: genius is as common as dirt, as abundant as dirt. And, what do we do to bring it out so that *everyone* enjoys receiving and giving of their genius? Everyone. No exceptions. None.

NORA: So, you've mentioned the word courage a few times… It sounds like you're finding integrity in the relationships between yourself and your students—not just the good, easy ones, but all of your students.

MADHU: Yes.

NORA: And, if I'm going to have integrity in this relationship, that means I'm going to have to have the courage to understand that everyone has this capacity for genius.

MADHU. And Joy.

And, honestly, teaching and learning can become pretty mechanical and joyless. It becomes all about performance and a grade. Do you know the interviews with Joseph Campbell and Bill Moyers (1988)? They are in a series called *The Power of Myth*. In part four of this series, which I happened to watch two weeks ago, Joseph Campbell is talking about how he teaches (when he was a professor many years ago). He would meet with each one of his students every two weeks, individually. And, what he's looking for is that conversation where, for the first time perhaps, the person sitting across from Joseph Campbell discovers what it means to follow their bliss. You know that expression, following your bliss? And it's exactly what I've been talking about. Recognizing what makes you so exceptional, what your genius is. Maybe, for most, it's not about reading and writing, it's about engaging in different things in different ways, etcetera. Joseph Campbell said, "Even if, after that 1-hour session, they fail to follow that bliss for the next 10–20 years because they're trying to get to the top of their professional ladder or whatever, there will be that seed that's been planted, that memory that's so authentic, so profound, so deep, that it's lodged there. And at some juncture in their life, something shakes them out of that automatonic life. And, they realize what it is to live with authenticity."

I don't know what integrity is without authenticity.

But, in a place, in a room, where people are masked and can't reveal their real self because they feel they aren't good enough or they feel they're going to be misjudged or they—you know, the usual. Very, very epidemic inferior complexes. Which I see in such *incredibly* intelligent people who still doubt themselves. Apparently, the biggest fear of Harvard graduates is that sooner or later someone will discover that they're not special, that they just lucked out.

So, I tell my students, "This is not about the stage, it's not about the grade, it's about being real." Being themselves, putting out what's important to their heart, their souls, their body. And, people have written *remarkable* things, *remarkable* personal stories. For me, this is what I look forward to reading. Because then I feel they don't have their cover-up, their mask, their whatever.

NORA: I hear you talking about the ways you're trying to draw out authenticity and find a relationship of integrity with the students. How do you answer that question of what makes you exceptional, what your genius is? How do you "follow your bliss?" Do you feel like you're doing that now and that this role, as an educator in this place, that that is part of how you would answer that question of where you find your authentic self?

MADHU: YES! I find my authentic self—which is really my joyful self—in this work. That doesn't mean I don't have sorrowful days, I don't have anguish, I don't have pain. And, I let students know this. Because they always say, "How come you're so joyful?" And I'm very clear that I have my share of carrying the cross. I have my daily challenges, my daily sorrows. But when I come here, I come to ignite the joy in them. I come from a place of joy. That doesn't mean they aren't allowed to be sad or to feel like they're failures. But, I'm not going to come out of a place of despair or hopelessness or mistrust. I'm going to come trusting in their best selves.

None of this is possible if you don't believe in loving. It's all about loving and about being patient. And about them really mattering, even if you're not going to see them after 14 weeks. Even if they're trying to jerk you around and tell lies. Even that. Even when they're being their *most* manipulative selves. I approach them with a lot of respect and affection—or at least I try to.

You do it by going overboard on being kind. In ways that they can't even believe they're being treated so well. They're in shock. You have to shock them with so much kindness. The Dalai Lama says, "My religion is not Buddhism; my religion is kindness." And what he does in saying that is so important in a world full of violence and hate. Hate crimes, hate crimes, hate crimes.

NORA: So, there's a real beauty in developing these kinds of relationships that help bring out students' passions and genius, and doing so nurtures a part of what you feel your calling is, or your authentic self.

MADHU: Yes!

NORA: And yet, it takes place within an overall institutional structure that is highly problematic and in some ways seeks to do the opposite of what it is that you're trying to do.

MADHU: Exactly.

NORA: So, how do you deal with that feeling—does it bother you or...

MADHU: Sure it bothers me! Some days I come back feeling like a fake! And why the hell am I continuing? But now that I know I've only got three semesters left [before retiring], I want to offer my *best*... in *very* difficult circumstances.

If I see you following you bliss, it doesn't mean that you have nice sleep and, you know, you're doing everything exactly the way you want to, but you're following your deepest impulse. I'm constantly inspired to look for my blissful self, to awaken my blissful self, to not bury my blissful self, when I'm in the presence of people who are themselves blissful. So, if students see me following my bliss, if they see me come to class filled with joy, and it can be an ice storm outside, and they see me celebrating life, and they see me celebrating *them*. Then at least—this is not just about theory—I'm living my bliss. With *all* the contradictions, with *all* my disappointments, with all my doubts.

Somebody who is alive will seek to spread life. Somebody who has been beaten down and beaten down by the system, will of course promote the system. So the question is how to set that spark, as Joseph Campbell says, that happens when you discover what your bliss is.

Are you following your bliss, Nora Timmerman? Ha ha!!

NORA: I don't know! I need to think about that!

MADHU: I'm just kidding.

NORA: Well, I do think about that. I have good days, bad days.

MADHU: Because you're a healthy, robust person living in a world filled with pain. We would be numb and dumb not to be aware of this pain. Right in our rooms, right under our noses.

NORA: Yes, absolutely. I have one more question that I want to explore with you. Once I started engaging in deeper analysis of all three portraits, I realized that I started the research with a very individual definition of integrity. I thought about integrity as the alignment between one's own values and one's actions—similar to the way in which Parker Palmer talks about it. However, after engaging in the research, I realized that there are other, more relational and collective ways of understanding integrity. Integrity can be thought of as lying within a collective project or effort toward some greater good. I heard you talking about it in terms of your relationships with your students, you find integrity by calling out your students to be their authentic selves, etcetera… What do you think about these ideas of individual and collective integrity? Do either have resonance for you?

MADHU: In a book that Gustavo [Esteva] (1998) and I wrote—Grassroots Postmodernism—we have an entire section: from an I to a we. To me, this notion of an "I," a disconnected "I," is such a weird idea. Again, I bring in Ivan Illich who says, I discover who I am in the people: the pupila of persons into whose eyes I look. And you know there's so many ways of saying it… I don't know how to find myself except in relationship to other human beings, to other creatures. I don't know what would be the meaning of love if there was just this atom. We're not atoms. We're part of Indra's net. And, our quest for self-knowledge is part of our quest to know the otherness of the other. And of course, I can get very Hindu, and finally, as they say, it's all one. You know, we're all part of this cosmic consciousness.

I tell you, we have such a capacity to give each other joy and we have such a capacity to give each other misery. And, I have faith and hope. There are the doomsday, apocalyptic people, whom Illich accuses of apocalyptic randiness. And, I just subscribe to the other, that we are all capable of awakening from our tiny little atomized selves to something larger, something more beautiful and grand.

***

New Questions

"None of this is possible if you don't believe in loving. ... You have to shock them with so much kindness." This quote from my dialogue with Madhu makes me smile the most. It feels so true to who she is; it reveals her. I think of it still when I'm with my students—ones that seem disengaged or that I feel suspect of some kind of manipulation. I am not Madhu, and I do not think my students would describe me as someone who shocks them with kindness, but there is something in her words and approach that challenges me in important ways. Whereas a default paradigm in formal school settings is to measure, evaluate, punish, or reward, Madhu's very nature casts that paradigm aside. She believes that everyone has the capacity for "genius," that everyone should "follow their bliss."

I've been trained well to shy away from words like "bliss." I worry that they are too optimistic, too essentializing, too "fluffy," even. But, I have immense trust and respect for Madhu. I hear wisdom in her words. Her question to me: "Are you following your bliss, Nora Timmerman?" was said in laughter, but was piercing nonetheless. I realize that part of the reason that it moved me was because of who was doing the asking. That is, Madhu was right. She said that she comes from a place of joy, from a place of acknowledging the "genius" in everyone, turning away from inferiority complexes. And, this is more than just nice words with Madhu. I feel that joy and trust she has in me when we talk. When I am confronted with this question from her, someone who has trust in me, someone who has joy (amidst the pain), I am not so scared of the question. I hear someone asking me to… well, find my integrity.

And as she asks me to find my integrity, I sit with the questions that her openness and authenticity have offered to my learning… How can I love all of my students? Treat them with so much kindness in ways that acknowledge how they all have capacity for genius? How can I engage my students and also my wider community in ways that help them to find their bliss? How can I use my work to bring awareness of the systems that make us complicit? In my life broadly, how can I separate shit from state? How can I think about integrity as boiling down to loving?

Notes

1 Happy Valley is a name used by locals to refer to the State College region of inner Pennsylvania. Penn State, a land-grant university, has been the hub of this region since its establishment as an agricultural college in 1855.
2 As of 2022 and the publication of this book, Madhu is now Professor Emerita at Pennsylvania State University.
3 Illich, I. (1971). *Deschooling society.* New York: Harper & Row Publishers, Inc.

References

Berger, J. (1984). *And our faces, my heart, brief as photos.* Writers and Readers.
Berry, W. (1987). *Home economics: Fourteen essays.* North Point Press.
Berry, W. (1990). *What are people for?* North Point Press.
Esteva, G., & Prakash, M. S. (1998). *Grassroots post-modernism: Remaking the soil of cultures.* Zed Books.
Illich, I. (1988). *The educational enterprise in the light of the Gospel* [Unpublished essay]. Retrieved July 14, 2020, from http://www.davidtinapple.com/illich/1988_Educational.html
Moyers, B. (Writer & Interviewer), & Campbell, J (Interviewee). (1988, June 21–26). *Joseph Campbell and the Power of Myth.* Retrieved July 14, 2020, from https://billmoyers.com/series/joseph-campbell-and-the-power-of-myth-1988/
Orr, D. (1992). *Ecological literacy: Education and the transition to a postmodern world.* University of New York Press.
Orr, D. (2004). *Earth in mind: On education, environment, and the human prospect.* Island Press.
Prakash, M. S. (2009). Rajinder's remarkable rasoi: What my mother's village kitchen can teach American schools. *Yes! Magazine, 49,* 48–50.
Prakash, M. S. (2011). Commons, common sense and community collaboration in hard times. *PowerPlay: A Journal of Educational Justice, 3*(1), 39–69.
Prakash, M. S., & Esteva, G. (2008). *Escaping education: Living as learning within grassroots cultures.* Peter Lang.
Prakash, M. S., & Stuchul, D. L. (2004). McEducation marginalized: Multiverse of learning-living in grassroots commons. *Educational Studies, 36*(1), 58–73.
Snell, M. (1995). An invitation to Ivan Illich: An enemy of conventional wisdom and a sage against the machine. *Utne magazine.* Retrieved October 10, 2012, from http://www.utne.com/archives/AnInvitationtoIvanIllich.aspx
Traven, B. (1966). Assembly line. In *The night visitor and other stories* (pp. 73–88). New York, NY: Farrar Straus and Giroux.

5

Ray Barnhardt

An Appropriate Case of Laryngitis

Taxidermied trophies and thick wood paneling decorate the walls up to high ceilings, hearty foods are on the menu, and we sit to order. This stop at the Fairbanks Pump House restaurant is my last in town before returning home. Nestled in this gold rush-style historic restaurant-saloon, Ray, his wife Carol, two visiting professors from New Zealand, and I discuss the events of the last week. One of the Indigenous professors from New Zealand gave a presentation the day before at the Alaska Federation of Natives conference titled, "The Role of Education in the Empowerment of a People." In it, he talked largely about the contribution of education to the "cultural and economic enhancement" of Indigenous communities. During dinner, as he discusses the sacredness of the land to Maori people, I ask him about his earlier presentation, "Don't you find that with today's forms of 'economic development,' there's inevitably harm to the land?" Right away he answers, "Yes, that's one of our dilemmas." And, after explaining various considerations and ways in which this dilemma manifests itself, he concludes, "We're looking for a middle ground: economic development through cultural means so that we don't degrade the land; there's a lot of challenges to that, but that's the goal."

That evening over dinner, I have many questions about these ideas and goals. I lean toward visions that seek non-capitalist futures, that critique the very notion of "economic development," as I see it being one of the largest roots of the same land degradation the speaker wants to prevent. Yet, I do not know this person well. He is an Indigenous Elder, me a young, white graduate student. Moreover, I had not yet extensively studied or immersed myself within struggles for decolonization and Indigenous autonomy. Perhaps if we were in relationship, we could dive more deeply into this critical dialogue. As it is, I choose to listen for understanding, mostly remaining quiet. It feels strangely fitting, then, that over the course of this last week I have spent in Alaska, I have had acute laryngitis. I stayed on the outskirts of gatherings to avoid passing on germs, and mostly observed people and places. When I did talk, it was in an almost-inaudible voice, hoarse from coughing, yet poignantly indicative of the uncertainty I had been feeling within.

Ray Barnhardt is also white, a settler in Alaska, born from second-generation immigrant parents. But, unlike me, he has made it his life's work to know about and work toward Indigenous autonomy in education. He has lived in Fairbanks, Alaska for more than 40 years and is full Professor at the University of Fairbanks.[1] Dozens of initiatives and projects list his name as collaborator with First Alaskan Elders, researchers, administrators, and teachers. In fact, even most of Ray's nuclear family has significant ties to First Alaskan education. Many years ago, when they first moved to Alaska, Ray traveled with Carol and their 2-year-old son to rural villages as a field researcher for a study on "American Indian education." Navigating the troubled waters of non-Indigenous research within rural Indigenous communities, having his family present—particularly his young son—"broke the ice" for Ray, opening the doors for trust and connection. Through family, Ray was able to begin learning about First Alaskan culture and forge relationships that continue to this day. At the time of my visit with Ray, Carol is the Chair of elementary teacher education for the University of Alaska Fairbanks (UAF). Their daughter, Amy, is an elementary teacher and adjunct professor of education at UAF. And Ray's grandchildren attend the place-based Watershed Charter School that bases its curriculum on the Alaska Standards for Culturally Responsive Schools. First Alaskan education is something Ray's whole family knows about in intimate ways, even if they themselves are not Indigenous.

And yet, my visit to Alaska reveals traces of uncertainty in Ray as well. It is difficult for me to get Ray to talk about himself. When I ask him about his own ideas or the challenges he faces personally, he tends to turn the conversation toward concrete examples of projects he has worked on, or if he does talk about ideas, they are often the ideas of others. This tendency seems partly indicative of Ray's immersion in Indigenous communities where relational, place-based, and collaborative understandings of knowledge are prevalent (Barnhardt, 2002, 2008a). Still, I think there is something else going on. Ray's disinclination to talk about himself and his ideas feels like a distant cousin to my own actual and metaphorical laryngitis. As a non-Indigenous person working in and with Indigenous communities, Ray must continually re-negotiate his own role according to the unfolding needs of Indigenous educators in their work toward autonomy. Ray's work, then, is largely about positioning. What I initially perceive as silence or uncertainty is at least partially attributable to a lived positionality of respect, deference, and humility.

One Step at a Time

Figure 5.1. ANKN Patch
A patch from the Alaska Native Knowledge Network (for which Ray is the Director) depicting the five main groupings of Alaska's many bands: Southeast, Aleut, Yup'ik, Iñupiaq, and, from the Fairbanks region, Athabascan. Source: Author.

The state of Alaska[2] is 1,717,854 square kilometers, roughly double the size of British Columbia and one fifth the size of the continental United States. Its vast array of mountainous, coastal, and arctic terrain is home to more than 200 rural villages, eleven distinct cultures, and twenty different dialects (Alaska Native Heritage Center Museum, 2011; Barnhardt & Kawagley, 2010). Beginning with somewhat small educational endeavors by the Russians starting in 1784, to widespread initiatives to "Christianize" and "civilize" children through to the early 1900s (Alaska Natives Commission & Alaska Federation of Natives, p. 7, 2010), First Alaskans were subject to systematic attempts to (as Ray says) "break down the whole cultural system and [impose] a whole other set of values, trying to do away with language, and so on." Moreover, severe epidemics were brought to Alaska in 1900, resulting in 25–50% of First Alaskans losing their lives (Wolfe, 1982). When the U.S. government granted Alaska statehood in 1959, one response from First Alaskans was to come together in an effort to protect their rights to the land, forming an organization called the Alaska Federation of Natives (AFN). The AFN continues to meet annually with the mission to "enhance and promote the cultural, economic and political voice of the entire Alaska Native community" (Alaska Federation of Natives, 2013). In early fall, when AFN meets, many other friends, groups, and organizations do too, taking advantage of having so many people together that otherwise live in very disparate parts of the state. I come to Alaska during AFN as well, following Ray through five full days and nights' worth of meetings with students, colleagues, friends and family: a PhD student retreat, potlatch at the hockey rink, Rural Education Caucus, a distance-education course, and the actual AFN convention and arts and crafts fair.

With more than forty years of work under his belt at the University of Alaska Fairbanks, Ray Barnhardt is the longest standing faculty member there. Lining the tops of all available surfaces in his office are plaques describing teaching awards and outstanding research contributions. The walls are adorned with beautiful gifts of various crafts that overflow out into the adjoining common space. If it is not clear from the dozens of people that I witness seeking him out for a quick hello, bit of advice, or catch-up on respective family lives, being in his office confirms that Ray does good work that makes a difference in people's lives, and they are grateful for it.

In various capacities, Ray's research, teaching, and service are geared toward shifting First Alaskan education over to First Alaskan hands, helping to ensure that rural education is relevant, culturally appropriate, and place-based. The duration of his commitment to Indigenous autonomy in education and the friendships and trust he has created along the way seem to keep him mostly relaxed and comfortable within this work. When critical questions do arise for Ray, they have to do with the ongoing negotiation of his role. He asks, "Where do

Ray Barnhardt | 93

Figure 5.2. Ray's Honors

From the top: four out of more than a dozen plaques honoring Ray; stretched hide with a map of the Yukon and Northwest Territories, the text reads: "Best Wishes from Teacher's College, N.W.T;" hand-carved baleen name plate; small-scale representations of the fishing trap and people of Old Minto, and a special plaque and poem for Ray's work within Old Minto. Source: Author.

I fit into an environment that is the Native cultural environment? What right do I have to enter into that domain, and what role do you carve out in doing so that isn't contradictory to the things that are the basic premises of what I'm working from?" And, while Ray finds workable answers to these questions, he does not rest for long in any of them. "I don't have a [definitive] answer to the question of where or how I should think of myself; it's kind of one step at a time."

Ray's CV is a testament to his shifting roles. Some academics, once hired within a tenure track position, may take on administrative roles in addition to their professorships, their changing roles tied together by the thread of their own evolving interests or personal career "advancement." Ray's professional commitments, however, are significantly varied and are motivated, not by self-interest, but rather by the changing needs of First Alaskan communities. In writing, Ray refers to this type of positioning as the work of an "advocate," someone who only takes on work that allows them to "keep in close touch with the community," who would be willing to choose losing their job over "alienation from the community," and who believes that change occurs "by bringing institutional practices into closer alignment with the expectations of the community being served, rather than the other way around" (Barnhardt, 2010, pp. 10–11).

Ray self-identifies as an advocate. He recognizes his privileged position as a white academic and endeavors to use that privilege in dynamically strategic ways. Most of the time, this results in him taking on the role of facilitator or administrator. "I've tried to be very careful to be in a position to facilitate and support initiatives or prepare [doctoral students] in a way that they have access to the range of tools and knowledge and skills and so on, and such that they can exercise greater control over their lives." Rather than taking on roles that position him as the primary researcher, author, or some kind of authority figure, his choice to work in administrative or facilitative roles shows his deference to First Alaskan control of their own needs, questions, ideas, and initiatives.

In the foyer of my hostel for the week, Ray stamps snow from his boots and lightly flaps his jacket. Glancing down the hall, I feel a notable twinge of shyness as I collect my belongings and go to meet him for the first time. Ray greets me with a quiet smile and holds the door as we step out into the gray morning. Minutes later we are ordering hot drinks from the second floor café of Ray's favorite used bookstore. Between sips, we exchange questions and answers, getting to know one another and setting up a schedule for the week. I am the first of his many meetings for the day. As we leave the bookstore, Ray gives me the lowdown on Fairbanks Elder Howard Luke, who we are on our way to pick up. Until last year, Howard kept up a home on the South side of the Tanana River.

Long after everyone else moved to Fairbanks proper, Howard continued to cross the river when it froze in the winter to maintain his home and relationships to the land there. After we pick up Howard, I get to hear stories from Howard's life firsthand over lunch. But before too long, it's time to go again and the three of us hop back into Ray's car to drive to the afternoon's main event, the Indigenous Studies PhD student retreat.

After personally greeting each person as they come through the door, Ray raises his fist to his mouth and clears his throat at the front of the classroom. The forty chatting people slowly face forward at their desks, away from the food trays at the back, the circulating tin of homemade oatmeal cookies, the 20' long relief map of Alaska pinned to the wall, and give their attention to Ray. He briefly welcomes us before standing aside and inviting Elder Howard Luke to give an invocation. Several minutes later, Ray briefly speaks again before standing aside to allow other administrators to introduce themselves. And after, he again sets up a series of stories from graduates of the program before stepping aside to allow them to be told. Literally and figuratively providing structure, then standing aside, Ray positions himself as facilitator and listener.

In other administrative roles, Ray's purposeful positioning has been even more evident. In 1994, he assumed one of the defining administrative roles of his career when the Alaska Rural Systemic Initiative (AKRSI), intended to increase culturally relevant education, was granted a whopping $10 million grant from the National Science Foundation and the Rural School and Community Trust. From the start, Ray and First Alaskan co-Principal Investigators Oscar Kawagley and Frank Hill, set up the grant so that it would be managed by the AFN. Ray explains, "Instead of the funding—ten million dollars!—coming to the university as the place where the expertise was... we arranged that the grant was submitted through the Alaska Federation of Natives. So the funding... came to AFN. It was the only time they'd done anything like this." After the politics of initial grant approval and then the approval of AFN as the recipient, "AFN sub-contracted with the Dept. of Ed, with the University, ... school districts, Native organizations, ... and so on. ... AFN was responsible, they were the ones who determined where the funds went, and we had to account for what we did with it." Over the course of the next 12 years and an additional $13 million, the project accomplished a significant amount in terms of breaking "down barriers between school and communities" and "increas[ing the] capacity of communities... to take control of the educational system." Ray attributes this success to have been built upon the strategic positioning of AKRSI at the outset: "[AFN] had ownership over the whole process. And it was that link that brought the

Elders into the mix… If [the funds] had been at the Department of Ed or university, it just would have been another mainstream, non-Native initiative. But because they had control over it, Elders came out of the woodwork, they were all over the place helping do this."

As he describes the initiative, Ray continually uses the pronoun "we." "What piece do you feel like you're bringing to these different initiatives?" I ask. In response, Ray stops for only a short half sentence to focus on himself before turning back to the story of the larger grant, its accomplishments and structure: "I've been in a position as administrator or director of the centers, or the projects and the grants and so on associated with this, but the work that was done through those [projects]… was a lot of people…"

When I talk with Ray's students, they describe characteristics that lend themselves well to his deferential positioning. A current Indigenous PhD student says that Ray is, "quiet, humble, dedicated… and possibly overcommitted." In reference to his humility, he adds that he "can see why [Ray] gets along well with Natives.[3]" Other students who have longer and more in-depth relationships with Ray describe him as "available, kind, and knowledgeable." Commenting in particular on how many people Ray knows and how much knowledge he has, one student taps his head and says, "He's got it all in here! … He's awesome, he's like a foundation, and he always credits others for the work."

Several days after our initial meeting and the PhD student retreat, Ray and I attempt to beat the midday rush that will accompany the lunchtime break at AFN, driving to a nearby diner early. Still, we just barely manage to get a table in the non-smoking section. Midway through my plate of fries and Ray's sandwich, he explains again that there is an iterative and unknown aspect to his professional identity. He says that one of his major considerations is "trying to focus my efforts on doing things that there aren't other people in a position to do at this point in time. When other people come along, PhD students in teacher programs, and so on, then I shouldn't be doing or pretend to be doing what they can be doing. So, over time, the challenge has been to try to identify what's the next component… [and] what's going to be the most relevant."

"How do you determine these 'components' and figure out what is needed?" I ask.

Hastily finishing the last bite of his sandwich, Ray pauses briefly before answering, "It's largely a matter of listening." He gives the example of the meetings with the new Indigenous Studies PhD cohort (almost all of which are First Alaskan) we had on Monday and Tuesday. Listening to their interests and desires for support as students, he is able to "focus on what students in the program need to know—writing, forming a research question, publishing an article," and so forth. The process of "hearing what frustrations, challenges, issues, students have and need help with… becomes part of setting up the support structure to deal with it."

At this point, Ray is still in a unique position to be able to help set up these kinds of support structures, but he senses that this time is coming to a close, and soon there will be less "things that I can bring to the table that aren't currently being addressed by somebody else." With First Alaskan PhD students graduating from the Indigenous Studies program and then turning around to be hired by the university, they are now in a position to do the type of administration, teaching, and research that Ray has done for the last four decades. Describing the doctoral program as "the capstone," he says it's "kinda like the last level at which I can make a contribution without feeling like I'm imposing an outside set of values."

"I'm the longest standing faculty member at UAF. I've outlived everybody else!" Ray says, laughing. "When I completed my PhD, I was 30, and that's when we moved up here. I moved around within the institution. I think this [Indigenous Studies] PhD [program] is probably my last project. Time to move on and do something else. I'm predicting that I'll be part-time teaching, be on [toward] retiring, at least see the students for whom I'm on their committee through their programs" within the next year or two. As his time shifts more fully from a professional to personal context, Ray's concrete projects will take shape more and more at home, and his accountability will shift to his family. With an ideal day for him involving some kind of manual labor and carpentry, Ray says that his yard is already dotted with some five or six homemade sheds. But, by now having become adept at re-negotiating his role according to the unfolding needs of his community (e.g. a wife fed up with so many sheds!), Ray chuckles as he assures me that, "Having the grandkids around takes the place of the next shed."

Relationship and Relevance

From the time Ray was a child, he has lived in cultural and economic contexts that foregrounded the importance of relationship and relevance to place. Ray was born and raised on a small farm in North Dakota that was originally homesteaded by his grandparents in the early 1900s. "We grew most of our own food. Eggs and cream were the source of funds to buy sugar and flour and things like that. … Everybody [in the community] worked together to help with whatever needed to be done. When it came time for harvesting, people got together and moved around from farm to farm to do the work because it was a lot of work with horses, and physical labor then." Ray can see the roots of his current work and ecological philosophy in his youth. He explains, "I felt an affinity with the physical environment as something that nurtured us, that we're an integral part of the environment, that we're not something that can be thought of as separate, aloof and above and controlling the environment. And I think that [these] views [or] inclinations that I have, grew out of my growing up on a farm and being dependent on it... seeing clouds come over the horizon and hail wiping out the whole crop for the season, the garden and so on, and trying to figure out how to eke a living out of all that. And watching my parents do that and not lose faith in the process. That our well-being, our livelihood, rides the waves of the environment in which we're situated."

Ray attended the same one-room country school as his father had; he was the only one in his graduating class. The connection between school and community was tight. "Curriculum was geared toward the things you needed to know to be a successful farmer in that area, so it was connected to the environment where we were living." The combined effect of a high school opening in a nearby town and the gradual replacement of physical labor with mechanical labor meant that Ray did not complete his schooling at grade eight, as his parents had. "The assumption or expectation was that we would follow in our parents' footsteps, but [the new] school opened new windows and doors and opportunities and perspectives. And then, conditions changed of course—machinery took the places of horses and a lot of the physical labor, and that meant you had to have cash and that meant you had to get into the economy." Once Ray finished grade 8, his parents rented out a small garage apartment that he stayed in from Monday to Friday while going to school, returning home to the family and farm on the weekends. Being the oldest of nine, he was the first to forge this path, but eventually all of his siblings followed, attending the same high school and boarding together in often overlapping stays at the garage apartment. Ray notes now that the transition his family went through from living off the land to a more industrial and capital-dependent economy is comparable to some of the changes Indigenous communities in Alaska have had to manage: "Very similar to what Native people are dealing with here, but in an agriculture context rather than a subsistence context."

Several years later, after a stint in the army and Bachelor's degree in math and education from North Dakota State, Ray came back to some of the educational principles of relationship and relevance to place that he encountered at the one-room schoolhouse. With his partner, Carol, he taught in an inner-city school in

Baltimore where the population was shifting from "semi-affluent white students to Black students" residing in social housing. The change in population density during this transition put extreme stress on local schools, forcing them to switch to a split shift in which one set of kids came for school in the morning and the other came in the afternoon. Further, the school had "no extra-curricular stuff… [it was] not a healthy school." Squeezing five classes into only half a day, Ray encountered the challenges of being extremely overworked and pressed for time, as well as cohort after cohort of students, unmotivated by curriculum that was mostly irrelevant to their lives. Thinking back to his childhood experiences of a curriculum that was integrated with his life outside of the schoolroom, he recalls, "I started experimenting with taking kids outside—using trig functions to calculate distance across the lake… That intrigued me because it wasn't the way my undergraduate education classes had prepared me to teach math, but I could see that you needed to have some way to connect what you were trying to teach with something that students could relate to, from their environment."

With Ray's interest in outdoor, relevant curriculum growing, he went on to pursue graduate studies. "[I] felt I had limited leverage in what changes could be made in the system as a teacher, but if I could become an administrator, I fantasized that I could have more impact." In an interdisciplinary doctoral program in educational administration and anthropology, Chet Bowers (2017) and Harry Wolcott (University of Oregon, 2020) helped add a cultural dimension to Ray's philosophy.

Given his rural upbringing in a subsistence agriculture context, it makes sense that Ray's academic work would have wound its way back to a philosophy that unites people and place. Still, though, his experiences on the farm are not an equal match to the history and depth of connection to the land that he encounters in his work with First Alaskans. Even after all his years spent with Indigenous communities, Ray is still "trying to understand and figure out what one does with understanding the depth of the relationship that people have with the environment, with each other, with the whole interconnectedness aspect of things." Several times during our week together he shakes his head and says with a smile how it's really true that "the more you know, the less you know."

"Cultures Have Literally Grown Out of the Land"

Our footsteps press quickly through crunchy snow. Ray has a meeting with a colleague in just a few minutes. Besides that, it's cold, and walking briskly just feels better. As we cross the Chena River, nearby ducks erupt in a fit of quacking and scatter away from the clang of our weight on the metal footbridge. Ray is talking about the historical trajectory of the field of outdoor and environmental education. He remembers how he initially sat on "outdoor" education committees that later changed their names to "environmental," and then to "ecological," most recently landing on "place-based." He explains how this shift in names reflects (for the field, but also for himself) a change in understanding around the role of culture in place. Whereas earlier iterations of outdoor and environmental education tended to separate nature from culture, prioritizing interactions with and understanding of the physical environment, more recent understandings of place-based education recognize the ways in which culture and nature are always, already connected in dynamic, mutually influential relationships (Gruenewald, 2008). There is an ecologist, Ray continues, who put together a map of discrete bioregions within Alaska, largely defined by watershed (Krauss, Holton, Kerr, & West, 2011). He then placed on top of this map another that showed discreet cultural groups, largely defined by language. Their boundaries were the same. Ray explains, "Cultures have literally grown out of the land." Place-based education for him, then, is teaching and learning about the knowledge and traditions that have arisen from thousands of years of life within particular places. However, we are not living in a world where that kind of place-based education is entirely possible, or maybe even desirable. We walk back across the Chena towards Ray's next meeting and the sound of our footsteps on snow end as we arrive at Ray's car, replaced by the whine of automatic gears and tires on a wide, salted parking lot. The combination of a walk along the Chena with the busy rush and structure of the day mirrors the tensions I see at play within the push for place-based education in today's rural Alaska.

The day after our walk on the Chena, Ray invites me to the Rural Education Caucus—a group of primarily First Alaskan policy makers, educators, youth, and Elders concerned with rural education. Discussions amongst these rural, place-based educators has clearly inspired Ray's thoughts. Never before had I seen "place" and "culture" used so synonymously. I am surprised by the uniform popularity of place-based education. Everyone at the Rural Education Caucus references it as if it is the undisputed goal of all 70–80 people in the room.

However, the stated goals and conceptions of place-based education expressed here differ from what I have often otherwise encountered. There is little to no discussion of mainstream "environmental" content based on consumerism, energy conservation, or recycling. Instead, place-based education in Alaska centers more on culturally appropriate curriculum and pedagogy. For instance, in Yup'ik villages, place-based education is the teaching and learning of Yup'ik traditions and practices through the Yup'ik language. Although the words "ecology" or "environment" are not always explicit, there is an underlying affirmation that First Alaskan cultures have, as Ray said, arisen from the land, and thus carry with them eco-centric worldviews and practices (Cajete, 1994, 1999; Hampton, 1995). At one point during the Caucus, the "Youth and Elder" delegates share a summary of their dialogue from the day before. In a visual poster, they show self-perpetuating relationships at the core of a series of 16 values (e.g. stewardship of the land, subsistence, etcetera). The four "pillars" of their vision for rural Alaskan education include: 1) Elders and family investment in the classroom; 2) Native teachers; 3) let the land be our classroom; and 4) [First Alaskan] language in the classroom. Ray's own writing further confirms what place-based education can be here and how it is synonymous with cultural education. He explains how traditional, Indigenous forms of education are "carefully crafted around observing natural processes, adapting modes of survival, obtaining sustenance from the plant and animal world, and using natural materials to make their tools and implements" (Barnhardt, 2008a, p. 120). And these skills are passed on through "demonstration and observation accompanied by thoughtful stories in which the lessons [are] imbedded" (p. 120).

Yet, in addition to the prevalence of this notion of culturally placed education, there is an equal (and for me sometimes puzzling and troublesome) emphasis at the Rural Education Caucus on the politically dominant values of accountability, standards, achievement, and job preparedness. Ray's analysis is that First Alaskans (along with many other Indigenous peoples) currently live within "two worlds," the place-based world they have known and co-created with the land for time immemorial, and the world imposed and forced upon their lives by colonization (Barnhardt, 2008a). The arguments in much of his recent writing on place-based education advocate for educational approaches that integrate both Western and Indigenous views and practices. Choosing a "glass half-full" perspective, Ray suggests that Western and Indigenous views and practices have histories of competition and antagonism (with clear power differentials in the equation), but now they are/can be "striving toward reconciliation through new structures and frameworks that foster co-existence rather than domination and exploitation" (Barnhardt, 2010, p. 1). Indeed, much of the work of the Alaska Rural Systemic Initiative was dedicated to documenting an increasing array of educational endeavors that "successfully" reconciled or merged Indigenous and Western knowledge systems and approaches (Barnhardt, 2008a, p. 122). Having said that, Ray seems sometimes more optimistic about a process of reconciliation than others. While he works to document successes, my visit also reveals keynote speeches dedicated to (capitalist) economic advancement and educational standardization, and all these place-based education-focused meetings occur indoors in non-descript, boxed rooms with abundant styrofoam and plastic waste. Ray writes:

> The specialization, standardization, compartmentalization, and systematization that are inherent features of most Western bureaucratic forms of organization are often in direct conflict with social structures and practices in Indigenous societies, which tend toward collective decision-making, extended kinship structures, ascribed authority vested in Elders, flexible notions of time, and traditions of informality in everyday affairs. (Barnhardt, 2008b, p. 157)

In today's neocolonial, climate-crisis context, efforts to institutionalize place-based education in Alaska thus find themselves in struggle. Functioning within these two worlds, working toward integration of two often-opposing frameworks, many call for a education rooted in Indigenous land and languages, and many also call for job-preparedness. Toward the end of the Rural Education Caucus, an Elder stands up to address the entire gathering, reminding us, repeating twice: "The real education is out there [pointing outside]. From the land, the ocean, and the air. The real education is out there. From the land. The ocean. The air." Admittedly, I find myself unsure: does he say this in support of the work happening here, or in contrast to it?

"Domesticating the Ivory Tower"

Skies are dark at the end of a long day. After a bit of dinner, four students, Ray, and myself join up in a small basement-level room that adjoins his office. Ray sets up a black polycom conference speaker and microphone in the center of the table. Shortly afterward, five cohorts of university students and faculty members from all over the world dial in to a phone conference. It is week nine of the course, "International Seminar on Cultivating Native Well-Being." Required for PhD students in the Indigenous Education degree program at the University of Alaska, it is co-taught by five faculty members, one from each of the international universities at which the course is offered.

It was back in 1970 that efforts began to "domesticate the Ivory Tower," what Ray describes often as bringing the university to the students instead of the students to the university (Barnhardt, 2002). The course we "attend" now, facilitated by distance education, is one manifestation of this "domestication." Across a wide array of programs (teacher education, Master's, and PhD), Ray has been part of projects that place students and teachers in the field (i.e. in domestic, rural contexts) for multiple purposes. He explains that a primary goal is for First Alaskan students—who can otherwise feel physical, cultural, and social isolation and disorientation in university courses and living arrangements—to be able to maintain their way of life and integrate their university education into their existing worldview. Ray further suggests that when students are at home, the pressure to conform to Western standards decreases and questions of how two different conceptions of the world may relate to one another increase. On the faculty side, the "domestication of the Ivory Tower" has created programs and courses that place faculty members in rural communities for both their professional development and course instruction. Ray's writing explains that these placements are intended to challenge the Western norms that separate those who produce knowledge from those who consume it, demonstrating through lived experience how much teachers have to learn and learners have to teach in rural Alaska (Barnhardt, 2002). Additionally, these efforts with faculty aim to increase awareness of the wealth and value of Indigenous knowledge that is often otherwise overlooked in dominant compartmentalized and abstracted university norms. All told, the more than forty years' worth of efforts to "domesticate the Ivory Tower" remain ongoing and, during my site visit with Ray, take shape in two very different courses. The first, this distance education course, is designed for mature PhD students with the goal of sharing scholarly insights and finding shared purpose and synergy across institutional borders among various Indigenous students and scholars (Barnhardt, 2008b).

At the designated time, voices start popping up. Everyone who connects says hello to Ray. In addition to being the instructor for the Alaska cohort, he is a central figure in the organization and connection process of the course as a whole. An abnormally long fifteen or twenty minutes are spent connecting, reconnecting, muting, and un-muting the speakers until everyone is on board. Finally, Hawai'i confirms, "Okay, Ray. Everyone's connected now!" And Ray exhales, "Alright, let's keep it that way."

Class begins by each cohort muting their microphone, with the exception of the instructor who is responsible for presenting that given week. Today, both Ray and the professor from Ontario are presenting. She goes first, and we mute our mic. Often, instructors or student presenters will upload powerpoint presentations so that they can be shared with everyone, but her powerpoint has embedded videos, and it would be too difficult to synch them all up, so we just listen. At

Figure 5.3. Alaska to Aotearoa
Video conferencing is also used during the PhD student retreat when we connect with the Indigenous Studies program in Aotearoa (New Zealand). Indigenous Studies programs in Alaska face significant challenges because of the sheer size of the state and the diversity of language and cultural traditions represented therein. Whereas the Maori students and faculty are housed together in an ornately painted and carved fare (traditional meeting house pronounced FAR-eh), speaking Maori, and singing songs, the Alaskan students gather in an unadorned conference room at the UAF. Although many introductions and thanks are said in students' native languages, our interactions are necessarily in English. Thus, the geographic and cultural diversity of Alaskan Indigenous students, alongside the typical structures of the university, necessitate different kinds of learning places and shared experiences than might happen in otherwise smaller contexts. Source: Author.

least I do. The other students seem to be occupied with their laptops, and Ray intermittently prepares for his part of the lesson, checking his powerpoint or glancing at a book. The Hawai'i cohort has forgotten to mute their microphone and we can hear them intermittently laughing and talking in the background. They speak exclusively in Hawai'ian.

When I first heard that Ray was teaching place-based education through distance learning, I admittedly raised an eyebrow. In one of our first email exchanges, I cautiously wrote, "It seems like it must be a fascinating challenge to teach place-based types of education over a distance!" Generally skeptical of technology, my eyes see tools that demand a particular conformity of bodies and minds, that quiet us, push us toward desks, tables, and screens. Even while technology enables real-time global communication, I wonder about the quality of that communication and connection. However, Ray's response to my questions, along with my experience in Alaska, gives me pause. In his email reply, Ray wrote, "Actually, by having place-bound students firmly embedded in their own 'places' while they are taking the distance ed classes, they are able to put PBE principles into practice and draw on each others' experiences to enrich the learning process." Further, he explains during my visit that, "Rural students, when they're in *their* own communities, are much more likely to challenge and present other views that make the class more rich" than when they are otherwise required to physically come to the university for a course.

Ray's words teach me something about my expectations for place-based education and the "domestication of the Ivory Tower." My expectations were initially more aligned with the Elder who spoke out at the Rural Education Caucus: "The real education is out there. From the land, the ocean, and the air." Yet Ray's clarity about how distance learning technologies allow people to remain embedded in their communities and raise critical questions they wouldn't otherwise have offered, is key. While institutionalized forms of education are colonial tools and have acted in colonial ways for centuries, Ray's work pushes back on racist norms that tend to associate Indigeneity with static forms of traditional technology. These are complex intersections. And while one example of Ray's "domestication of the Ivory Tower" is this online course with the Indigenous Education PhD students, his second example is strikingly different, and one that he describes as the "most rewarding."

The technologies used in Ray's second example of domesticating the Ivory Tower are salmon traps and birch bark baskets. For the last 20 years, Ray has been taking groups of public school teachers to Old Minto, a fishing village on the Tanana River that has been used by Athabascan people for thousands of years. When Ray talks about the course, his conversation slows and he finds words harder and harder to come by. "You get to know people, Elders, at such a level… It makes me appreciate even more the phrase 'the more you know, the less you know.'" As opposed to the online distance course for (primarily Indigenous) PhD students, this intense 3-week summer course is designed for non-Indigenous students. The goal is to increase cultural awareness, or at least—as Ray explains— to increase the *capacity* for learning from and with First Alaskans. The hope is "that they will be able to and comfortable [with] entering a new community and knowing how to go about learning about that community and understanding that community from the perspective of the people that are there." Together, Ray and the students spend about 8 days camping at Old Minto. While there, the "only" job they have is to live. Off the land. Salmon need to be caught and traps repaired. Canoes need to be made, songs sung, and fires lit. There are no lectures or powerpoints here, nor are there concrete learning outcomes or even set roles for who is a teacher and who is a student. At Old Minto, living life is learning, there is no distinction.

Ray says, "I just tell people, it's your responsibility to figure out what's going on and to connect with people in ways that you can participate and be a contributing member of that place and get to know the people there and for them to get to know you. ... So we don't have meetings—sometimes we do if there's an issue floating around or the Elders want to talk about why things are happening. You have to figure out how to negotiate your way into whatever it is you want to do. ... I participate just like them, we're all on the same plane; I'm not a faculty member at that point. ... The Elders each have their own skills and roles that they play and we join in, become part of that. So, they're living their life the way it comes naturally in that setting, and we become part of it, amazingly so."

Participation in a subsistence lifestyle offers tremendous, yet subtle lessons not only for students, but also for Ray. He says, "[I will] only appreciate years later what I either didn't recognize or I thought was by accident, and was actually deliberate. ... It takes a lifetime to reach a deep enough layer that you're not violating their way of doing things." In a context where learning happens through living, perhaps the most significant "outcomes" of his own experience are the relationships created. Old Minto has given Ray a real sense of belonging: belonging to people—he is regularly invited to ceremonies, funerals—and belonging to the land. When the time comes for his ashes to be spread, he wants them to be dropped at the head of the Chena, flowing past Fairbanks, "into the Tanana [next to Old Minto], then into the Yukon, and then the Bering Strait... going past all the places I know and love."

The very notion of "domesticating the Ivory Tower" thus walks a meandering line between the "two worlds" of traditional subsistence education and modern, institutionalized education. The non-Indigenous students that are immersed in the Old Minto "cultural camp" are preparing for the cultural context in which they will be teaching. The Indigenous students in the PhD seminar are in a more "modern, institutionalized" course that spans local *and* global Indigenous contexts, promotes digital *and* face-to-face relationships, and is both instructor *and* student-led (two-thirds of the course is made up of student and community-led presentations versus the instructor lectures I witnessed). Each in their own way, these courses are working to meet the needs of multiple communities within,

Figure 5.4. Chena With Moon
The Chena River, flowing through downtown Fairbanks at sunset with a full moon rising.
Source: Author.

what Ray aptly describes as, "an ever-evolving complex, adaptive educational system and cultural milieu." He further suggests that,

> It has been through the interplay of teacher, learner, and researcher across diverse cultural contexts that new constructs have emerged and new educational opportunities have been generated—the ivory tools on the tundra have begun to blend with the literate traditions of the ivory tower. (Barnhardt, 2002, p. 247)

The projector screen lights up during the second half of the PhD seminar. We all turn to watch as Ray's powerpoint is shared and he begins his lecture. He describes the changing role of higher education in Indigenous communities over the last 30–40 years, outlining a new initiative for accreditation of Indigenous universities, colleges, and programs. Because he is sharing this week's timeslot with the professor from Ontario, and because of the earlier technical difficulties, Ray only has five minutes for questions before the "thank yous" and "goodnights" start to filter in from the international cohorts. Once only the Alaska group remains connected, they spend another half hour discussing students' final projects. Ray's advice to virtually everyone is to aim for relevance: consider how it is "relevant to your future teaching, to the course topic, and to similar issues others are also dealing with… start from the place that [you're] in, use local knowledge." Tired from the long day, we collect our belongings and bundle up in anticipation of the cold night air, say goodbye to the two Alaskan students remaining on the conference call, and Ray turns off the black polycom speaker.

Integrity in Collective Commitment

Coming to know and spend time with Ray surprised and challenged me in many ways. If questions about contradiction, complicity, and integrity inspired the visioning of this project, I leave Alaska with yet more questions. However, in Ray's situation of being non-Indigenous in First Alaskan contexts, I find that the question of complicity shifts to a question of commitment. Ray cannot live according to a First Alaskan philosophy because he himself is not (nor would he pretend to be) Indigenous. He accepts and utilizes this position as a moral compass of sorts, guiding his advocacy, helping him know where and when to help, and where and when to step back. Ray's subsequent ease, his many accomplishments, and his trusting relationships stir up new questions about community, dedication, and humility. How might integrity be more than a personal virtue, how might it exist amongst a people and in a place, in a collective commitment to what is good for those people and that place?

***

Dialogue on Integrity and Complicity

At the time, Ray's portrait challenged my assumptions about integrity in substantive ways. What I saw in my time with him was a sense of integrity that stretched beyond the self, out into a community and into a purpose. I saw integrity as something that *we do*, not just something that *I have*. And, because of Ray's sense of integrity as something that lies in shared goals, his portrait illustrated the importance of relationship and positionality. For Ray to have integrity, he must continually tend to and assess his relationships with First Alaskan Elders, students, colleagues, friends, and family, and tend to the role he assumed within those relationships.

Ray taught me about how my initial conceptions of integrity were individualistic and permeated by a white, urban sense of environmentalism, despite my best efforts to try otherwise. Yet, his teaching was indirect; he taught by living, through example. Profoundly humble, Ray only set out to share what he learned from others, to highlight their work, but in doing so, he taught not only about what they say, but he shared his own ethos.

Ray's attention to relationship, community, and positionality shifted my sense of integrity so that, when I went back several years later to engage in dialogue with all three participants, I asked each of them about their views on integrity as a collective project…

***

RAY: When I reflected on some of the questions you're proposing for this interview, I couldn't avoid feeling deeper appreciation for the contributions that Oscar Kawagley made both to our programs and to my work specifically during the time he was with us. The work I did with Oscar drew me away from the administrative side of things and toward the philosophical and ethical side of issues related to integrity. So, I was looking at a book called *Moral Ground: Ethical Action for a Planet in Peril* (Moore & Nelson, 2010) this morning. This book showed up just a few months before Oscar passed away. And, even though I worked pretty closely with him on much of his publishing, I didn't even know that he had submitted a chapter to this book. It arrived in the mail one day, and there were something like 80 authors listed on the back as having contributed to it. It was people like Wendell Berry and the Dalai Lama, Scott Momaday, Pope John Paul. And I looked and my eyes caught sight of Oscar's name, with all these people. So, I turned to the short piece that he had done. And, within that chapter, there is one paragraph that, more than anything else that I've written or others that I've associated with, captures some of the core insights that you were asking about. It provides a sounding board for much of my own reflections and thinking. And if it's okay with you, I'll read this short paragraph (from (Kawagley, 2010, p. 218):

> We, the Yupiat, believe that the Ellam Yua (God) is in Nature. Therefore Mother Earth has a culture. This is why we as Native people emulate nature. We see God in Nature and know that everything that Nature has made is a vehicle for teaching us how to make a life and a living for ourselves. Our subsistence way of living is a process of actualizing a lifeway that encourages altruism. Altruism requires

that we give utmost respect and honor to everything of Nature, as each element does its job as required by the Ellam Yua.

The notion of integrity for me ties directly into the kind of work that Oscar and people like Harold Napoleon and Howard Luke did. And, just, of course, being with a whole group of people that made their insights accessible to others through DVDs or books. Between Harold and Oscar, they gave voice, they gave Native voice, to the work that we were doing and provided a grounding that, for me, speaks to what you might want to call integrity, integrity being the connections between ideas and actions. And, the actions that I tried to adhere to are those which strengthen the voice of Native people and put them in a position to take on issues from their own point of view, from their own Native perspectives on education and all that.

NORA: That reminds me of one of the pieces that I ended up focusing on in your portrait, and felt like I learned from you in terms of this concept of integrity. It seemed like you had a practice of wanting to be in a facilitator, administrator position where you weren't the one who was generating all of the decisions necessarily, or the kind of creative thinking of the program, but you were leaving that up to other people with the goal of having First Alaskan autonomy over their education.

RAY: As Frank Hill put it, Oscar was the dreamer, and I was the schemer. That was a role that I felt I could legitimately take on, and a place where I made some contributions while Oscar was dealing with the dreamer complexities and insights that helped breathe life into the documents and programs and so on.

Right before Oscar passed away, we had been working on putting together a couple of books. We also currently have lots of classes being offered around the country. The number of activities that I have been engaged in in the last few years, these two charter schools, for example, the Effie Cochran charter school, which is a culturally based charter school, and the Watershed charter school, which is a place-based school. The cultural standards work and the efforts to develop guidelines that provide avenues for educators to use cultural standards in ways that are meaningful for their work. The Cross-cultural Studies PhD Program. And, we were directly and indirectly involved in the Declaration of the Rights of Indigenous Peoples as well. All of these projects provide avenues for making the insights that people like Oscar and Harold shared, directly reflected in schools. They also provide a framework for doing the kind of work that we're talking about as far as getting Native people into the forefront of shaping research, shaping policy, shaping educational practice, and so on.

So, all those things which have emerged in the last few years have taken the work that was done previously and tried to put it together in a way that people could make use of it. We intend to avoid useful insights from being stuck on the shelf somewhere, we want to make them available for people to use or pass on.

NORA: Cool. Ray, it seems to me that there's a tension, and I have very limited understanding of this, so, I apologize in advance if I'm just being ignorant here. It seems to me that there's a tension that your written work with Oscar has highlighted between Indigenous and dominant, instrumental, Western worldviews. And, those differences in worldviews shape the social structures and institutions as well. So, how much of the work is bringing Indigenous people into the existing structures that have emerged from these western, Eurocentric traditions, and how much of it is not working within those structures at all and resisting them in the work toward more Indigenous autonomy and sovereignty? I'm curious about whether you sense that tension, how you work with it, and how you see other people working with it. How does it play into this discussion about contradiction and complicity and integrity and things like that?

RAY: The approach that I've taken, and Oscar as well, is not to replicate what's there and put a native name on it, but come up with alternative ways, as Graham Smith (2003) has put it, to develop transformative processes that re-frame and put things in a different perspective. And, we're in the middle of it. One of the very strong influences that Oscar had was in the framing of Native ways of knowing in a way that brought into question other ways of knowing. So, it wasn't that we were arguing to do away with Western psychology or Western ways of knowing, but the approach that we took was to put out new and different, alternative ways of making sense of the world and framing the changes in ways that people come to understand or appreciate them on their own without all the time making arguments or being on the defensive. In other words, we were trying to be on the offensive.

On the administrative side, what I attempted to do over a series of several years, was to really frame how we think about the whole administration and management, policy making, and so on, using a framework that was developed by a person named Antony Wallace (1970). From a cultural perspective, he described how the administrative process needed to be shifted away from the "replication of uniformity" and toward an "organization of difference" that embraces diversity.

Reading his work helped define where I might focus my efforts on the impact that administration has, and how to facilitate in a way that reinforced the value and significance of diversity.

NORA: Do you feel that you've been successful in that way? Have you had times where you've felt like, "Oh, I'm not sure how much I'm doing that, how much am I working to create something new instead of replicating, or, how much am I working toward diversity instead of replication?" How have you negotiated that, or has it felt pretty strong?

RAY: All these efforts—the Alaska Native Education book, the Moral Ground, the PhD program, the cultural standards—are drawn from engagement with not just individuals, but a whole collective of individuals who were bringing this brand-new light into something that had been dormant. And, we decided that we would know if we are achieving what we set out to achieve if the people that we're working with—Elders in particular—come back a second time, or a third or fourth time. And, if they participate and contribute and share and build on, that they're finding enough insights for their own lives and their identity and so on, that they're willing to take the time to participate and join in.

Also, I'm thinking of the Sharing Our Pathways book. We organized the book by cultural region, and when we were working with Elders down in Kodiak, they became very engaged, and you could see that they were sharing the ideas and experiences that they had. But, they were concerned that people wouldn't understand or misinterpret the points that they were trying to make, that their meaning wasn't necessarily self-evident, and this was exacerbated by the fact that they shared ideas that weren't final, they were still grappling with the insights. So, this led to those Elders in Kodiak putting a hold on the information that they had acquired and accumulated, they weren't ready to share it yet. What they did agree to was that the documentation that they developed, acquired, or built upon, was something they wanted their children and grandchildren to know, to learn, to understand. And, what we worked out with them was an arrangement where we put their work on a password-protected website so that their children and grandchildren could have access to the resources and ideas without those being misunderstood by people, non-native people. So, it was a matter of collaborating in a way that the goal that the Elders wanted to achieve could be achieved without sacrificing some of the risks associated with doing that. And actually, about five years into it, they were ready to share it. It's now on the web, and if you connect, you can access it from anywhere.

NORA: Well, it sounds like—and maybe you can tell me if I'm summarizing this right—it sounds like your goal has been to work with others who are providing a space for the various Indigenous groups within Alaska to continue passing on their knowledge, their insights, their goals for the future, and that education is one place where that can happen, and so you're trying to utilize these spaces—these educational spaces—to do that work as best as possible, in the ways that fit with what Elders want, using whether they're showing up and participating as a guide to tell you if this is what they want, and you're following in the right way. Is that right?

RAY: Yes, you captured that very well. I consider my role is to find ways to make sure that the insights were accurately documented and shared and used in ways that communities were comfortable and Elders were comfortable.

NORA: Okay. Well, I will definitely write about the importance of process and relationship when I put this together, as well as your discussion of Oscar's influence, because that sounds like it's an important piece to include. Is there anything else you wanted to say that you haven't yet?

RAY: Well, the only thing is to reiterate how it's the insights that Harold and Oscar and all the others that are associated with this, and continue to be associated with it, it's their insights that give life to this work. Harold Napoleon's (1996) book, *Yuuyaraq: The Way of the Human Being*, and Oscar's books have been by far the most in demand, re-printed numerous times, distributed all over the place. And it's been very rewarding for me to have had a small part in helping get these books published and seeing how they have taken on a life of their own. But, the substance of that didn't come from me, the substance came from Howard and from Harold and Oscar, and others. My part was putting it out there.

NORA: Cool. Wow. Well, I continue to be in great admiration of your work, Ray. I know that you deflect compliments and credit for it, but it's really inspiring.

RAY: Well, thank you. I am just a piece of the puzzle, a part that contributes, I'm not in control of it.

***

New Questions

Ray returned again and again to the notion of himself as the schemer, the facilitator, the assistant, or organizer. He helped Oscar, Howard, and Harold's work get into print, then into classrooms, then into the foundations of the Alaska Cultural Standards for education. Yet, in this final interview that I had with Ray, he shifted his focus slightly.

While he continued to position himself as deferential, as "just a piece of the puzzle… not in control of it," he opened the curtain to his passion for the theory, the purpose, the creative control, and the vision of the "dreamer." The one thing he emphatically shared during this interview was the paragraph from Oscar's chapter in *Moral Action for a Planet in Peril*. This paragraph does not discuss how to be a good facilitator, schemer, organizer, advocate, or assistant. It paints a vision of a people. In sharing it, and in saying, even though it was just once, that his relationship with Oscar shifted him from less of an administrative to more of a philosophical role, I got a sense that Ray is pulled by and passionate for this vision of what it means to be human and alive in Alaska. Not only is Ray interested in First Alaskan autonomy, he sees, feels, and has love for First Alaskan worldviews.

Ray's discussion of structural change was interesting to me. In general, Ray's writing and his interviews tend to point toward a both/and approach to integrating Indigenous and Western structures and ways of thinking. He finds an appreciation and role for both, and despite the differences, thinks that they can be integrated in a way that maintains diversity to the benefit of people and place.

He still avoids the discussion or sense of complicity or contradiction. It seems to not hold much resonance for Ray. Importantly, this bears no connection to whether he is still critically engaged with questions about how to live an ethical life. He absolutely has—what he calls—a "moral compass" that guides his decision-making and informs his sense of integrity. Ray's relative ambivalence about whether and how he is complicit, and the way he is able to disconnect complicity and integrity has helped me re-frame my own story about integrity. How is integrity a meaningful, guiding concept outside of whether it has any connection to, or anything to bear on one's complicity? Ray's answer to this question is firmly rooted in relationship: it is meaningful when you have deep relationships to people, places, and cultures, and your actions are in service of maintaining their wellbeing. Today, as I reflect on the learning I have done with Ray, I ask myself where is my power and how can I use it to change the structures that marginalize and oppress others? When I embark on this work, who am I partnering with? Can I partner with those who are most impacted by those marginalizing structures and thereby amplify their work? And most concretely, most importantly, how are my actions serving my most meaningful relationships?

Notes

1. As of 2022 and the publication of this book, Ray is now retired from his professorship at the University of Alaska, Fairbanks.
2. The very notion of a "state" or "province" imposes colonial forms of power (in the shape of borders, boundaries, rules, etcetera) on Indigenous land.
3. Most Indigenous and non-Indigenous people I encounter at the AFN, Rural Education Caucus, and in the Indigenous Studies PhD program at the University of Alaska, Fairbanks, use the words "First Alaskan" or "Native" when refering to Indigenous folx from the Alaskan region. In this case, I am directly quoting an Indigenous student of Ray's, and in other cases throughout the portrait that are my own writing, I adopt the language "First Alaskan(s)."

References

Alaska Federation of Natives. (2013). About AFN – Alaska Federation of Natives. Retrieved January 12, 2013, from http://www.nativefederation.org/about-afn/

Alaska Native Heritage Center Museum. (2011). Cultures of Alaska: Education and programs: Alaska Native 2012. Retrieved January 12, 2013, from http://www.alaskanative.net/en/main%2Dnav/education%2Dand%2Dprograms/cultures%2Dof%2Dalaska/

Alaska Natives Commission/Alaska Federation of Natives. (2010). Report of the education task force, 1995. In R. Barnhardt & A. O. Kawagley (Eds.), *Alaska native education: Views from within* (pp. 7–30). Alaska Native Knowledge Network.

Barnhardt, R. (2002). Domestication of the ivory tower: Institutional adaptation to cultural distance. *Anthropology & Education Quarterly, 33*(2), 238–249.

Barnhardt, R. (2008a). Creating a place for Indigenous knowledge in education: The Alaska Native Knowledge Network. In D. A. Gruenewald & G. A. Smith (Eds.), *Place-based education in the global age: Local diversity* (pp. 113–133). Lawrence Erlbaum Associates.

Barnhardt, R. (2008b). Indigenous knowledge systems and higher education: Preparing Alaska Native PhDs for leadership roles in research. *Canadian Journal of Native Education, 31*(2), 154–166.

Barnhardt, R. (2010, December 13–17). *Indigenous contributions to sustainability*. Paper presented at the American Geophysical Union, San Francisco, CA.

Barnhardt, R., & Kawagley, A. O. (2010). Culture, chaos, and complexity: Catalysts for change in indigenous education. In *Alaska Native education: Views from within* (pp. 199–216). Alaska Native Knowledge Network.

Bowers, C. (2017, January 21). *Introduction*. https://cabowers.net

Cajete, G. (1994). *Look to the mountain: An ecology of Indigenous education*. Skyland, NC: Kivaki Press.

Cajete, G. (1999). Reclaiming Biophilia: Lessons from Indigenous Peoples. In G. A. Smith & D. R. Williams (Eds.), *Ecological education in action: On weaving education, culture, and the environment* (pp. 189–206). Albany: State University of New York Press.

Gruenewald, D. A. (2008). Place-based education: Grounding culturally responsive teaching in geographical diversity. In *Place-based education in the global age: Local diversity* (pp. 137–154). Lawrence Erlbaum Associates.

Hampton, E. (1995). Toward a redefinition of Indian education. In M. Battiste & J. Barman (Eds.), *First Nations education in Canada: The circle unfolds* (pp. 5–46). University of British Columbia Press.

Kawagley, O. (2010). Extra! Extra! New consciousness needed. In K. D. Moore & M. P. Nelson (Eds.), *Moral ground: Ethical action for a planet in peril* (pp. 217–219). Trinity University Press.

Krauss, M., Holton, G., Kerr, J., & C. T. West. (2011). *Indigenous Peoples and Languages of Alaska*. Fairbanks and Anchorage: Alaska Native Language Center and UAA Institute of Social and Economic Research. http://www.uaf.edu/anla/map

Moore, K. D., & Nelson, M. P. (Eds.) (2010). *Moral ground: Ethical action for a planet in peril*. Trinity University Press.

Napoleon, H. (1996). *Yuuyaraq: The way of the human being*. Alaska Native Knowledge Network.

Smith, G. H. (2003, October). *Indigenous struggle for the transformation of education and schooling*. Keynote address to the Alaska Federation of Natives (AFN) Convention, Anchorage, Alaska, U.S. http://www.ankn.uaf.edu/curriculum/Articles/GrahamSmith/

University of Oregon. (2020). *Harry Wolcott*. https://anthropology.uoregon.edu/profile/hwolcott/

Wallace, A. F. C. (1970). *Culture and Personality*. Random House.

Wolfe, R. (1982). Alaska's great sickness, 1900: An epidemic of measles and influenza in a virgin soil population. *Proceedings of the American Philosophical Society, 126*(2), 91–121.

6

Educator Vignettes

Nine experienced and insightful educators from Canada and the United States wrote the vignettes in this chapter. I gave them the extreme challenge of writing about their own experiences of complicity, contradiction, and what integrity means to them within seven to eight hundred words. I asked them to both share their conceptual understandings and illustrate those with personal stories, and I asked them to do so in a format that would be public and non-anonymized. While I solicited these stories, provided the frame and guiding questions, and worked with these folks editorially, the vignettes in this chapter are composed of their words and their writing. The wisdom and the beauty of their stories belongs to them. I ask the reader to please also recognize that the framing of the prompt was mine, and thus any critique of the premise of their vignettes should likely be directed to me, not them. Additionally, as with all of us, we are complex, multitudinous beings that are in flux. These vignettes were written years ago and represent mere glimpses of ideas and experiences that surely have continued to evolve.

Tracy Friedel

Many years ago now, in carrying out a Masters study focused on Indigenous parental involvement in an urban public school, I came to wonder how, in the context of settler colonial legacies of disenfranchisement through schooling, Indigenous students might reclaim cultural practices called for by Elders; lifeways that had served their Ancestors well in terms of proven and trustworthy knowledge translation techniques. I set out soon afterward to explore this topic through a PhD study. In so doing, I was gifted a very valuable lesson at the hands of the Indigenous youth who joined me in that experience.

Together, the youth in my study and I spent most of one summer plus part of a fall engaged in activities that were part of an Indigenous-focused place-based learning study. The premise for the research came from a statement often made by Elders, *"To know who you are, you must know where you come from."* At the culminating research interview in the fall, I asked the youth to tell of the place that held the most meaning for them from among all those we had visited over the course of our time together. We had traveled to many places over the preceding weeks, often times accompanied by *nêhiyawi* (Cree) and *âpihtawikosisân* (Métis) Elders. Our travels took us to sites of historic significance, places where cultural ceremonies were hosted, traditional territory that we crossed in canoes, etc. In answer to my query regarding the most significant place … literally all of the youth identified our rented 15-passenger van as holding the most meaning for them. It was the van that transported us between locations and according to these young people, it was more than a transport vehicle. It was a significant 'place,' steeped in remembrance. In identifying the van as 'place,' youth upended longstanding assumptions found in a great deal of the place-based learning theoretical literature, namely that the concept of place and 'the outdoors' are mutually exchangeable, or synonymous. This teaching led me to experience first-hand the limits of Western perspectives for understanding Indigenous-centered teaching and learning. Or as Eber Hampton (1995) describes it in his own PhD study, this finding helped me to "clear the underbrush in my own thoughts about Indian education" (p. 5). Notwithstanding that Indigenous students are often thought to benefit from time spent "out of the classroom," this experience called for a more nuanced cultural understanding of innovations in place-based learning.

Growing up *nêhiyawi* (Cree) and *âpihtawikosisân* (Métis) in west central Alberta, I had attended all-White public schools where there were not only few opportunities to understand what it meant to be *nêhiyawi-âpihtawikosisân*, there was also significant danger in identifying with that cultural heritage at all. In that regard, I could closely relate to the youth in my PhD study who spoke of the racism that runs rampant still in Canadian prairie cities, and of the ensuing difficulties to learn *"where you came from"* within the public school system. Like them, I was lucky to have had family connections that provided some elements of this learning outside of the formal school system. A takeaway from my PhD research, notwithstanding recent efforts to create space for cultural approaches to teaching and learning, seems to be the notion that Western schooling and Indigenous pedagogy are naturally misaligned.

Education (including outdoor education) continues to be largely premised on non-Indigenous ideas and structures, and thus limited in terms of meeting the important objectives of cultural revitalization and self-determination that are the focus of many Indigenous students, parents and communities.

In my PhD study, I had hired white outdoor educators specifically for the purpose of teaching core outdoor/environmental education components. An early assessment by these educators was that the Indigenous youth I had recruited were not interested in learning at all, that they were too distracted by each other to focus on the skills and knowledge (e.g. rock climbing) being taught to them. As the research progressed, it became evident that youth were exhibiting less of a resistance to learning than they were acting on core teachings they had received from Elders. Not necessarily cognizant of the language of social determinants of health, owing to their engagement with Elders in their home communities and elsewhere, youth were keenly aware that their well-being was founded upon a deep sense of social belonging, and that there are important links between this and the idea of living well in place.

Youth actions correspond with core values that lie at the center of Cree teachings, for example, the importance of relationships. Each of these young people exhibited a nuanced sense of their social selves as lying at the heart of what it means to be embedded in place in integral ways; kinship/place connections are an important continuation of a holistic and persistent Cree worldview. Their identification of the van as 'place' was simply confirmation of this deep understanding.

Kinship/place connections are also evident in the processes associated with learning to pick sweetgrass, an activity that we participated in during the summer portion of the research. Such ritual is highly reliant on being guided by Elders to locate the plant using sight, smell, feel, and other senses, on offering (tobacco) to the land as giver of the plant's life, on harvesting only that which is needed and no more, on leaving sufficient plants to ensure future propagation, on sharing one's harvest with others, etc. This type of social bond, between youth and Elders and with the plant itself invokes notions of reciprocity and obligation to community. This level of intimacy and understanding regarding the negotiating of relationships and managing of the environment is central to upholding the peoples' cultural identity. The young people in my study were alive to this meaning, cognizant of the important of maintaining integrity across multiple spheres (e.g. biological, ecological, spiritual, social) both for themselves as individuals and themselves as members of broader collectives.

With the lessons learned from my PhD research and as a university teacher, today I aim to disrupt outdated student perceptions regarding Indigenous peoples' culture, history and knowledge. Mainly, I have done this through focusing on the concepts of place, land, territory, and so on. It can be quite a foreign experience for students to encounter knowledge that is produced in non-Western ways, through embracing the deep subjectivity inherent to both observer and observed, and in the context of the animate and inanimate. Yet, if we are true to our aims as Indigenous educators, we must do this very thing. Indeed, it is through such engagement that one comes to understand one's place in the world and the concomitant obligations associated with that relationship. Again, *"to know who you are, you must know where you come from."* This is true whether we live in rural or urban areas, are raised by our birth family or others, etc.

Now more than ever seems the right time for shifting our curricular focus (formal, informal, non-formal) so as to more closely align with the interconnected thinking that lies at the heart of the cultural knowledges of Canada's First Peoples. For Indigenous and non-Indigenous Canadians alike, the recent Truth and Reconciliation Commission calls to action (Truth and Reconciliation Commission of Canada, 2015), Canada's adoption of the United Nations Declaration on the Rights of Indigenous Peoples (United Nations, 2008), and general uncertainty regarding species survival in an era of accelerating climate change make this an urgent need. In response, many universities have recently created mandatory Indigenous education courses for pre-service teachers that aim to advance efforts to 'Indigenize' the curriculum. The struggle for me personally in relation to such courses is that they tend to be driven by the university's own corporate aims and standards of institutional integrity, and not the ethical and relationship commitments I am called to adhere to as an Indigenous person. I worry that such courses can tend to be premised on outdated and simplistic assumptions about Indigenous peoples, and that by boiling down Indigenous experience to an easily digested 3-credit course, we largely ignore the pervasiveness of settler colonialism and situate Indigenous educators in a contradictory position, making it difficult for them to address the ongoing impacts of White history. The result of the mandatory course is that we may be short-changing real opportunities to advance Indigenous epistemologies through the whole of the university experience.

My work increasingly focuses on understanding how to support communities in restoring dynamic place- and land-based cultural teachings that center spiritual and physical relationships. And I still focus much of my work on Indigenous youth. It is not that I don't care about what it is that pre-service educators are learning. It is just that so much of this latter work seems to be happening in contexts where Indigeneity itself is being increasingly objectified, resource-ified and materialized in order to better align with new technological advancements and downward pressure on institutional budgets. These core tensions are sure to occupy much of my time and energy, and that of my colleagues, in the years ahead.

Connie Russell—We Spend our Privilege

In the early 1990s, I began to consider pursuing a PhD. I struggled with the idea partially because I had a titch of impostor syndrome. Mostly, though, I worried that doing so would take me too far from my activist intentions. The urge to "make a difference" by fighting oppression and fostering social change was a guiding force in my life and is intimately bound up with my own interpretation of living a life of integrity since I seek congruence between my actions and my desire for a world where we all—human, more-than-human, and the land—can flourish. My MES supervisor encouraged me to broaden my understanding of what counted as activism and convinced me that scholarship is, in fact, a vital part of any social movement. The academy has indeed been a good fit for my passions and skills, yet I also have encountered challenges to my integrity, many of which are wrapped up in the enormous privilege and power I have as a tenured academic in a Canadian university. In my teaching, research, and administrative work, I aim to "spend my privilege" using the leverage points available to me. The results have been mixed.

As a teacher, I have sustained contact with a group of folks explicitly gathered to learn together. I teach courses in environmental, social justice, and interspecies education and have witnessed the ripple effects as my former students go on to influence others as teachers and social change agents. Yet I admit I have also unwittingly reproduced oppression in my teaching—through reinscribing racism, settler colonialism, fatphobia, ableism, speciesism, and neoliberalism, as examples. Thankfully, identifying these contradictions is integral to my pedagogy, and

I try to model being grateful rather than defensive when students bring them to my attention. My scholarship is similarly driven by my desire for social justice and environmental flourishing, but I sometimes wonder how much of a material difference it actually makes. What *is* useful research? How do we know if our research has made a difference? These questions remain unresolved for me.

Perhaps because I have had fewer opportunities to process the experience, I am most troubled by the contradictions I faced in my work as an administrator. I was a department chair for five years and an acting dean for one. In those roles, I was able to lead a number of exciting initiatives such as ensuring environmental education, Indigenous education, and social justice education be integral to our BEd and MEd programs. Doing so enhanced my sense of integrity. Still, in some of my actions as an administrator I also consented, in the Gramscian sense, to the ongoing neoliberalization of the academy, which I would argue is counterproductive to social and environmental justice. No single moment stands out as being particularly egregious but taken together they add up in a worrying way.

For one, I found myself working far too much, especially in my year as dean. I already have tendencies towards workaholism so this was not terribly healthy for me personally. I also think it sends the wrong message to others about what it takes to be "successful" in the academy. I also often found the work stressful, especially when assisting students or colleagues in crisis and addressing incidences of oppression. I was unable to emotionally disengage as some advised I ought. By the end of my six years in administration, I was burnt out. Two years later, I still shudder at the thought of returning to administration while at the same time, in what is arguably a gendered response, I feel selfish and guilty for declining requests to do so.

I also am hesitant to return to administration given much of my time as an administrator was spent leading program reviews, completing reports, and pulling together numbers to support various proposals. Sometimes I could see the benefits of doing so, but oftentimes it seemed like an awful lot of work to reach a foregone conclusion. I thus tried to be strategic, putting some tasks on the back burner, refusing to do others altogether, and prioritizing those I thought would best achieve my goals. Even so, I worried I was nonetheless consenting to an audit culture that I find counterproductive. Audre Lorde's words about the master's tools never dismantling the master's house echoed in my ears.

And there were some things I failed at as an administrator. While I managed to secure a few new full-time positions, the number of new hires was insufficient to replace departed faculty and the plight of adjunct faculty did not improve sufficiently under my watch. The reliance on contingent labor in the neoliberal academy is a widespread problem and bound up with systemic issues like underfunding of universities and the rise of the managerial class. Tenured faculty are also complicit. When I raise the plight of adjunct faculty with my colleagues, I find most express sympathy but few seem willing to share what they consider to be their hard-earned gains. I am unsure how to proceed strategically with integrity on this front.

I have been following Sara Ahmed's "killjoy" blog recently, curious about her decision to resign her tenured faculty position over her university's failure to adequately address sexual harassment. Her action raises questions for me. Would I make more of a difference from within or outside the university? While I believe my skills are best used in an academic setting, is that just a story I tell myself because I lack courage or imagination, or because the material comfort of my position leads me to resist digging too deeply? How do I address the many contradictions in my life that undermine my sense of integrity? How do I balance the need for self-care with my desire to spend my privilege and make as much of a difference as I can? I seek ways to both push myself yet be more gentle with myself.

Richard Kahn

For almost twenty years now, I have worked as a critical educator/theorist who seeks to produce social and ecological justice through the advocacy of veganism, defined by the Vegan Society as "A philosophy and way of living which seeks to exclude—as far as is possible and practicable—all forms of exploitation of, and cruelty to, animals for food, clothing or any other purpose." While many vegans see veganism as an individual lifestyle politics primarily concerned with making enlightened consumer choices, I understand veganism as a demand for collective change, towards which individual transformation is a necessary but not a sufficient condition. My understanding of veganism is thus both radical and somewhat uncommon and most folks that self-identify as vegan with whom I engage as an educator or activist generally do not share my revolutionary approach. Indeed, I often find that they are happy to feel morally empowered through their vegan identity, which they imagine as an individual reform that allows them to improve society via the removal of animal products in their (and hopefully future others') lives.

Despite apparently having a less systematic approach to the philosophy than myself, many vegans I meet seem far more absolutist in their thinking than am

I. For instance, I have not infrequently witnessed people who, by identifying as a vegan, have felt free to belittle or shame others for (ab)using animals by maintaining diets based on meat or dairy, using leather, or supporting other cultural activities (such as going to the zoo) that might be considered wrong from a vegan perspective. Sometimes the people who are subjected to vegans' scorn are themselves serious social justice workers, vegetarians, or environmentalists who have otherwise politicized their lifestyles, and often their communities at various levels, in other progressive ways.

In such cases, without seeking to dismiss the critiques of my fellow vegans thereby, I will ask them critical questions designed to point out the systemic contradictions and hypocrisies of veganism. Human beings are obviously animals as well, thus veganism should be committed to anti-oppression and peace-building approaches across cultural groups. Hence, I will ask other vegans about how much they do to exclude the sufferings of other people. Sometimes, in response to this, I am told that veganism is not about animal suffering but about the suffering of nonhuman animals due to speciesism. Here, I ask others to consider if maintaining moral concerns for nonhuman animals over and above those of human animals is not itself a speciesist position. Additionally, I may ask whether all vegans have equal experiences as a class. Do vegans of color or LGBTQ vegans or other vegans of lower socioeconomic status tend to receive and functionally work with the same cultural benefits as their white, straight, affluent counterparts, for instance? Alternatively, I may ask about how much they do to exclude and counteract systemic forms of harm to animals. Are they vigorously anti-war and military—documented to be the most overt harm to animals globally? Do they drive and condone the mass transportation system that results in at least hundreds of millions of preventable animal deaths per year? Do they eat grains or farm products provided by Big Ag, which also accounts for untold deaths of ground rodents, birds, bees, and insects? Or, I may ask about whether they eat out in non-vegan establishments or purchase food or other products created by machinery that also produces animal-based items, either of which is liable to cross-contaminate their vegan goods with at least trace amounts of exploited animal flesh?

Never a day goes by in which I do not myself seriously contemplate these and similar matters, seeking thereby to force myself to try harder to resist the dominant culture that encloses me despite my best efforts. For like all other vegans I am subject to—and in some cases even relatively privileged (as a well-educated, white American man) by many of these same contradictions—the point being that these lived contradictions manifest ultimately not due to individual error but because of the complex interplay between the present moment's utopian aspirations for freedom and justice (here named as veganism) and the real socio-political conditions that serve as the foundation from which the dream of veganism emerges as an emancipatory alternative. Whether limiting or benefitting us, the contradictions between the articulated dreams for peace, freedom, and justice and the ways in which our lives participate in blocking those dreams represent the theater of our moral progress or regress.

As a critical theorist, then, I am bothered by socio-political contradictions but also know that they are historically necessary aspects of our social development, as they constitute the grounds from which we can learn to become more humane as we try to abolish that which contradicts our ecological well-being. Rather than practicing "either/or" forms of thought that conceive of contradictions as the outcomes of failed understanding, I instead believe we need to promote dialectical "both/and" forms of thought that seek to recognize both the positive and negative aspects of our lives as systemically inter-related. The more we yearn for a sustainable world, the more we perceive the myriad ways in which our lives in society block sustainability. But rather than see the idea of sustainability as meaningless, because it is contradictory, a dialectical thinker sees that by actively organizing to oppose that which contradicts our understanding of it, we can make the world *more sustainable* and thus we can sustainably develop our world. Therefore, veganism (as with all other historical liberation and justice movements) must manifest as a contradictory endeavor through and through—and, as such, I see it as a *process of historical improvement* in which we attempt to consciously enact the ways in which our ideas and practices can better reject the dominant order that violates nature (both externally and our own).

Until the domination of animal nature ends *in toto*, we can never truly achieve a perfect veganism. This means that there are reasons to have more empathy for others' (i.e. non-vegans') contradictions, as well as for our own failures to live uncompromisingly just lives. For even as we appear to resolve one apparent aspect of our socio-political contradiction, its systemic nature means that it likely generates new contradictions for us to deliberate upon and change (e.g. the previously identified "hypocrises" of contemporary veganism as it is often practiced). Even as we seek to organize and educate one another through the identification of our mutual contradictions, I do not think it means however that we should tolerate them. In my own life, I strive hard to name the contradictions I find myself daily involved in and then, instead of arriving at guilt or shame, I attempt to foment critical action on these same problems whenever and wherever they arise.

Is the academy a vegan-dominant space and institution? Hardly. But it is *more so* because I work within it as an educator and theorist providing outspoken leadership on these matters. Can one be identified as white and vegan in a non-contradictory way? Likely not, and yet tethering my veganism to a commitment to being the best anti-racist educator and citizen I can arguably represents the historical arc of veganism in the present moment. Can I enact a vegan philosophy as a man within a society that is pathologically patriarchal? Yes, but not purely, and then only as someone who seeks to promote veganism as an ecological feminism concerned with the animal standpoint and the need for alternative performances of more sustainable identifications of what constitutes masculinity in the culture. And so on and so on. It is a learning exercise in how to become through the collective exercise of opposing that which prevents us.

Sean Blenkinsop—Paradox and Place: The Perils of Searching for Integrity

Thinking about integrity, my own in particular, has been a challenge. For instance, I don't recognize within myself the necessary sense of angst, implied by some of the book's framing questions, with regard to maintaining my integrity while living and working as a committed environmental education activist in the academy. I find this discrepancy between the implied and my own lack interesting and have decided to examine why I don't feel this angst, and also how I think about and try to live according to my sense of integrity, for it is an important concept for me. I'll divide this self-examination into two parts: place and paradox.

Part 1: Place ... *I was about 12, paddling in the camper canoe due west into the setting sun across the enormous expanse of Trout Lake. We had been in the boats for at least eight hours, and my companions had their heads down in that exhausted, it's-all-I-can-do paddler mode. We could see for several miles in all directions. There was not another soul visible (this was before the days when camps worried much about supervision), and the lake was calm and colored like molten glass as the sun extinguished itself in its waters. The three of us had not spoken in hours, and it was clear that my partners wished to be somewhere, anywhere, else. But my heart was soaring. This was the place for me, the place to be, the way the world should and could be, and better yet, is.*

Part of the challenge of integrity rests in the question of ends; against what standard is integrity being measured. Often, for those environmentally oriented, the measure is taken against an as-yet-not-achieved end. For example: I should not be doing X (where X involves flying to conferences, eating meat, working in an unjust/anti-ecological institutional setting, benefitting from the profligate destruction of nature, etc.), because X is not part of a Y (where Y is a way of life that is decolonized, place-based, equitable, care-based, eco-centric, etc.). And yet, for the person in question, the aimed for Y does not actually exist. Nor do the cultural boundaries, the complex set of structures, and the behavioral norms exist that might allow one to avoid doing all these problematic X acts. As a result, it is impossible for a single individual to align X and Y. If Y is the measure against which one's integrity is determined, it is difficult, well-nigh impossible, not to always fall short.

However, for me, there has always been a place in the present that allows me to be the best me I can be in this imperfect world rather than compare myself to an ideal to which I aspire. And that place is on trail in Canada's boreal forest. So, like Nietzsche's Zarathustra I can always escape to the woods, rejuvenate, ground myself and confirm again my own integrity after having compromised with and been complicit in the modern world dominated by human exploitation. The forest is one example of an eco-friendly, even just, environment to which we have access today.

Part 2: Paradox ... *I was 18 years old, a new undergraduate, when I happened upon a sign that was inviting volunteers to get trained and then spend several hours per week visiting with prisoners in what was, at that time, the most notorious maximum-security prison in the country. Over the course of three years of visits I came to understand quite clearly that each of these men, and I worked with up to 35, was a caring, interesting, relational being just like me. I also came to recognize that every one of them had killed at least one other human being which seemed quite unlike me. Yet overtime I understood that this complexity of good and evil could exist together without being contradictory within a single individual. I also, in a moment of honesty, noted that all of us, including those who have not murdered, are complex, convoluted and even paradoxical beings. In fact, by the end of the three years I realized that finding ways to acknowledge and live with the paradox that is our lives is both what makes me free and makes life interesting.*

For existential philosophers like Sartre or de Beauvoir, life is not clean, there is no right answer for every question, and often there can two or more contradictory but correct answers at the same time. Camus takes this concept of the paradox even further suggesting that there is a human desire towards order, towards making everything explainable and understandable. Yet, the universe in which we live is not actually orderly in this way. There isn't a clean set of answers, ways of being and doing, against which to measure our own behavior that would serve as a means to evaluate our own integrity. Thus, Camus concludes that we must find a way to live in this space between the order and the chaos, what he names the absurd. But, and this is where my own integrity lies, we must make the best decisions we can given the complexity of the situation, the limits of our own understanding of the way we want to be in the world, the knowledge we have to hand of the current situation, and the range of possibilities that are both allowable and that we can imagine. And we must take responsibility for those decisions. It is against this responsibility-taking that my integrity is judged, rather than against some correct, even perfect decision that reflects an ideal universe.

To bring Place and Paradox together, I start with the assumption that living is complex, conflicted, incomplete, and likely paradoxical but that I must choose to act in, and take responsibility for, ways that best align to the life I seek to live, and that no matter how challenging that process is within a western, neoliberal, market-capital driven, non-environmental institution, there is always a place where maintaining my integrity is easier, and that place involves lakes, trees, and rocks.

Heesoon Bai

I used to be very angry with people for poisoning the environment. I used to even think, in my moments of despair, that humanity deserved to be wiped out for poisoning the earth. For, we are the "cancer cells" (McMurtry, 1999) in the Earth Body. And according to the conventional medical paradigm, we need to poison (chemotherapy) and kill (surgery) these cells. Now, moments of anger are still there with me, but they don't consume me. My own slow maturation as a human being has taken the form of better understanding human psychology and learning to examine my own mind and heart, and seeing the Three Poisons at work.

As a student of Buddha's teachings, I see the current level of deadly and still increasing environmental degradation and destruction to be the work of these Three Poisons: greed (*moha* in Pali), aversion or hatred (*dosa* in Pali), and ignorance or delusion (*lobha* in Pali). These poisons seep into the core humanity and corrupt and destroy its integrity. Integrity, as the etymology of this word ('integrity' comes from Latin, *integer*, meaning, 'intact') shows, is a condition achieved when an entity is purified of corrupting materials that interfere with, complicate, and compromise its integral or intrinsic functioning. From the perspective of Buddhist psychology, then, integrity speaks to our intact humanity. Purified or detoxified of the poisons, we awaken to our essential humanity or awakened heart-mind (Bodhicitta) and reclaim our integrity as human beings. Learning to detoxify these poisons is a deep and difficult work, given that we ingest them every day in the form of dominant belief and value systems, ideology, media sound bites, the advertisement industry, lifestyle, and so on.

I am an educational philosopher or philosopher-educator. Adopting Raimon Panikkar's working definition of philosophy as having three interconnected aims of knowing, loving, and healing, and also infusing these with the Buddha's teachings, I see my work in the academy as helping others (students and colleagues) and myself, to see or come to know the Three Poisons at work within and without, and to heal ourselves through skillful love, known in Buddhism as the *Four Immeasurables*. The latter comprises of human emotions or states of being characterized by lovingkindness or friendliness (*metta*), compassion (*karuna*), empathic joy (*mudita*), and equanimity (*upekka*). When we can abide in these states of beingness, we are naturally free from the Three Poisons. This work requires committed practice: moment-by-moment, we commit ourselves to practice the *Four Immeasurables*. Since we have been ingesting the Three Poisons all our lives, and poisons are all around us, we can well imagine how difficult it would be to undertake detox and to practice these *Four Immeasurables*.

One of the fundamental principles of Buddhist ontology is interdependence and interpenetration: everything in the universe is completely intertwined, intermingled, and thus is infused through and through. Hence the Three Poisons we experience within us are manifest in the outer, physical world. The poisoned Earth is a collective manifestation of humanity at large. Knowing this, I'm acutely aware of my own complicity and participation in environmental degradation and destruction. Just by virtue of being born into and growing up in the culture and value system, I have ingested the Three Poisons, and have been spreading around and sharing them, even if at a minimal dosage. Knowing this, would I be condemning others—my students and my colleagues in the academy—and be angry towards them for their contribution to environmental degradation and destruction? The logic of "they should know better" does not apply to human psychology. If we knew better, we wouldn't have done what we did. The work before us is for each of us to detoxify ourselves and help each other detoxify. This is an educational work. This detox work is what moves us from being part of the problem to becoming part of the solution: *from complicity to integrity.*

From delusion that I'm an ego self, independent of all other beings, greed and hatred arise. For, if I'm a separate self, then I must put myself above all others in looking out for myself and taking care of my welfare. In short, I am in competition with all others, and since we all are in this situation, the competition we face is severe and merciless. I even compete with myself. I can never be content with what I have achieved or accumulated. I can never have enough. The blood of greed is constantly coursing through my psychic vein, and my heart that has no sense of "enough" knows no peace, and pumps faster and faster … until I collapse maybe with a heart attack. This delusion of being ego selves is, ironically, shared by everyone. If we can just deeply reflect and dwell on this irony, we may wake up to the reality of interdependence: every one of us is more or less laboring under the illusion of an isolated, separate, independent self. If we can properly appreciate this irony, we would weep and laugh and hug each other. We would feel so much compassion and love for each other, and we would be able to laugh together, rejoicing in solidarity and companionship. No more aversion, no more greed. Mutuality rules. We support and collaborate with all beings, including humans. This, I would present, as the ultimate environmental education curriculum.

Thus, for me, teaching in environmental education is not separate from, or different from, teaching in moral education, and neither of them is separate from teaching human developmental psychology. When I first realized the connection between moral education and environmental education, I promptly made environmental concerns the center stage of my moral education course. More recently, having studied psychotherapy, I now see an intimate connection between human developmental issues, such as attachment wounding and rupture (that includes ruptured relationship from Nature) and our inability to extend care and responsibility to environment. Our growth as ethical beings and moral citizens is one piece with our maturity as human beings. When we are not deluded about our individual ego selves as separate from each other and from all other lives on the planet; when we are not deluded that who we are, how we are, and what we do is separate from the affairs and well-being of the rest of the world, this is when we truly realize that we are "in it" all together. *Your* and *their* suffering (joy, too) affects *me*, and I suffer (and rejoice) with you and with them (all beings). This, I would present, as the ultimate environmental education pedagogy.

Laura Piersol

I recently returned to a place in the Canadian Rockies where I had lived and taught. I hadn't been back in ten years and decided to walk on a trail that had been a favorite of mine. As I walked it seemed as though I was encountering myself as it was those ten years ago, frozen in time. It was as if the place—the contours of the trail under foot, the mountainside facing me and the scent of lodge pole pine—were all holding that piece of self. The process of walking was like going back in time, bumping into vivid thoughts and feelings from when I had lived there. This encounter of juxtaposed selves, current and past, seemed to clearly be showing me what I had gained and lost in that time. I was able to feel at once all of the myriad ways in which I had changed in that time and out of that, both growth and loss were clearly distilled for me. In ways it felt as though the mountain was holding me accountable, all the large and little compromises I had made along the way in academia—teaching indoors too often, spending time on the screen much too often, backgrounding the more-than-human voices under pressure of focusing on human-centered concern—I felt keenly aware of these lapses in terms of what I hold dear as integrity. I realized how much I judge my integrity on the ability to attend to the natural world as a teacher.

I felt in that moment on that trail that I was "answerable" to the mountain, to the pine and to the soil underfoot. Bakhtin (1990) argues that a person's actions are ethical when they are "answerable" to the one who "addresses" them. Being "answerable" according to Bakhtin (1990) is more complex than being responsible, rather than simply accepting one's part in a scenario, being answerable means one's actions are open to being affected and changed by another because one has allowed themselves to be "addressed." In other words, they have been open to the possibility that the other might change their own worldview/perspective. When I am living with integrity as an environmental education faculty member it means that I'm embodying this openness. I'm trying to be aware of both how I'm being addressed and how I might answer in a way that allows the more-than-human to flourish and teach.

A key lesson that I learned on that mountain walk is that the natural world teaches me how to live with integrity if I listen. This is the tricky part, how do I make sure to make that time to listen and learn? How do I best encourage my students to do so as well? I have learned a lot about listening to the natural world through my own research (Blenkinsop & Piersol, 2013; Piersol, 2014) but it's a matter of making sure to embody these lessons on a regular basis. It seems that vigilance and prioritizing are essential here. Remaining hyper aware of all that pulls me away from the more-than-human and to make it a priority to resist this turn away. In effort to prioritize, I am trying to schedule meetings in the day with the ocean, the cedars, as I would with human co-workers. I am also trying to plan my lessons in the place where they will actually take place so that the more-than-human can actively be involved in the design. I've also begun to ask some particular questions so that I can maintain vigilance. These include: How might

I best attend to the natural world as co-teacher? Is my agenda/lesson here getting in the way of what the place has to teach? What voices, ways of being/knowing are silent, ignored and how might I foreground those? What is our impact on this place?

Palmer (1998) suggests "By choosing integrity, I become more whole, but wholeness does not mean perfection. It means becoming more real by acknowledging the whole of who I am" (p. 14). The whole of who I am is relationally embedded in the natural world. Within academia, I feel pushed to forget or ignore this, as though I should just be able to partition off these connections that inform and shape me. Teaching with integrity then feels like doing the best I can to care for more-than-human relations through attempting to be "answerable" to them. Interestingly, this work also pulls me deeper in relation with the maple, the slug, and the salal. Being connected to the whole of who I am also means being explicit with my students about the endeavor and importance of including the natural world as co-teacher, being "answerable" to that world, and also the struggle in trying doing so. As we do 'required' activities, we discuss how we might be backgrounding the natural world and think into ways around this. Living in line with my philosophies and values in this way means that I shut up and listen more and get out of the way so that more-than-human others are no longer the 'setting' for the learning but active teachers full of lessons I could never adequately teach.

The more-than-human world communicates and is always addressing us, offering perspectives that might bump up against ours. How do I "answer" as a human being? How might I ethically respond in return? The mountain hike that day was nudging me to ask this, and I'm still trying to live in a way that is "answerable" to the calypso orchids, the red squirrel, and the aspen.

Rebecca Martusewicz

I came to higher education teaching and scholarship first as a curriculum theorist via the work of people like sociologist of education Philip Wexler and philosopher of education Bill Pinar. I identify as a teacher educator most of all since I work in a former normal school, in a Social Foundations program within a Department of Teacher Education, and I embrace the work I do with practicing and prospective teachers. As is fairly typical of Social Foundations scholars, my work began with a focus on race, class, and gender via the disciplines of sociology, history, and philosophy. But sometime in the late 90s, I began to come to terms with a difficult realization: that I had been sublimating a deeper set of questions and commitments that were being refocused toward more acceptable social justice issues. That is, I had been taught since I was a little girl to stop asking questions about why we treat the natural world—animals and trees, marshes, rivers, and forests—as if they matter less than human life, as if we have some sort of natural right to decide their fate. Sometime around 1997, I began to press myself to face my oldest, most heartfelt concerns and questions. I began to read and write about an ethics that defines human life as inseparable from and responsible for our active membership in a network of complex and diverse living systems. And I began to see education as defined by that ethics.

This meant really coming to terms with all those years of apologizing for my "hyper-emotional" response to all the violence I saw being done to other creatures, and trying to articulate what I understand to be the roots of both social and ecological violence in the systems and structures of our culture. I think that is when I began to live from an authentic integrity, when I stopped apologizing as if I was somehow wrong to want to defend and care in these ways. My life changed. I entered a whole new set of scholarly friendships and collaborations, and community commitments. I began seeing differently and working differently. I went to Detroit to learn about the incredible community work in neighborhoods being done there to clean up abandoned factory lots, and feed families. I learned about how white, male, and human supremacy intersect as defining discourses in our lives. And, I learned what activism means when we can see a larger social, economic, and political context as it violates both human and more than human well-being, when we understand that we can never be outside nature, that we are in it and of it. And, I began to teach from my heart and from these scholarly and community endeavors. That is what integrity means to me: to live from authentic questions, to work hard to understand, to constantly question what we do not know, and to encourage others to do the same. It's about developing an ethics that can never be finally finished, that's about learning to care and respond in the face of others' suffering, to be able to experience joy from others' joyful successes, and to always recognize how small we are in relation to everything else, that we can never know enough to finally figure it all out even as we work to make life more livable.

I think integrity means trying to live and act and work in ways that respond to these ethical issues, and the questions that arise from them. Of course, our questions shift and change as we enter new relationships and learn from them, and so our work may change too. Before coming to terms with what I was ignoring in myself, I had questions that were defining what I was doing. I was working from certain principled positions, and trying to stay true to those, so I suppose there was integrity in what I was doing. But I also knew I was nagged by issues that I was not willing to face for a very long time, and once I did, everything shifted. Staying true to those twists and turns, embracing them even while we realize that they will shift again is also what integrity means.

This process has required, of course, that I work on myself as I work with others in the world. I can be quite judgmental and direct, so learning to rein that in and be compassionate and humble as I face my own faults and my own failures has not always been easy. I have never been one to sit quietly in the face of institutional or interpersonal problems. I can be quite opinionated and direct; something some of my colleagues have let me know is off-putting (especially from a woman, I am sure). I can't say I've necessarily succeeded in quieting that part of myself, and somehow this too—this willingness to speak up—is part of staying true to a set of ethical principles. But, I have learned to be more patient and I still work on timing and tact.

I think integrity includes learning patience and how to raise appropriate questions or issues. This process is especially important in my relationship with students. Because I recognize that we are all born into this culture and its logic of domination, I know how hard it is to let go of the myriad fantasies of superiority that shape our patterns of belief and behavior, policies, institutions, day to day interactions. Breaking through those ways of being (including our sense that we will never be good enough), means having the patience and kindness to teach concepts carefully, to ask students what happens to their worldview when they apply those ideas to the phenomena in their lives, and to be there when they breakdown or when they fly into a rage, or when they effervesce with the excitement of recognition or affirmation. Learning to teach as I too undo my own carefully protected heart and let myself feel the horrific damage being done in the world, is about developing the sort of integrity and courage needed to do this work. This is not a simple linear process and does not happen overnight. Trying to step up as we face what needs to be done both develops and requires a kind of integrity. I guess I mean that we start from a set of principles that help to define an ethical position, and then we work to respond to the world in ways that stay true to those principles. The principles define our integrity but so do the actions we take as we respond. And failing at it, as despair or fatigue or hubris overcomes what's needed, is part of the process too.

I know I suffer, as do we all in various ways, from the wounds of racism, sexism, anthropocentrism and other forms of supremacy even as I work to teach about their devastating effects. Interrupting internalized supremacy discourses is constant hard work. I worry a lot about my just-beneath-the-surface fears when meeting men of color on the street, or my sometimes stumbling and fumbling when trying to talk with African American or other colleagues of color. I catch myself being tongue-tied and feeling stupid in the presence of respected male academics. I have been stuck in more than one abusive relationship with a man. I know I cannot do enough in my own personal life to relieve the animal suffering that I see everywhere. I want to bring home every neglected, suffering dog I meet and I nearly careen off the road or put my husband through the windshield to avoid squirrels, chipmunks, and other small creatures.

I constantly feel the despair of not having enough time, energy, resources, or know-how to address these issues in my own community. I feel like I fail as an activist everyday. But going on in spite of this despair is also part of what it means to try to live with integrity: staying true even while we fail. Allowing ourselves to learn with and from others (including more than human others) and realizing we need to shift our practices and refocus or refine our principles yet again. Getting up and trying again. This is a complex process with no recipe for how to do it. It is all about the quality of the relationships that we form with others, and our willingness to care, be humble, respect limits, respond with compassion, and be kind as we recognize that we exist only because we are members of an extravagant and fragile living world.

Dilafruz R. Williams

"My life is my message." This Gandhian dictum has guided not only my personal life but also my professional life. Aspiring to be true to myself in *how I live* and *what I profess*, I am guided by a number of core values, three of which I want to address here: service, social justice, and sustainability. I regularly reflect on the meaning of my existence and on ways my East-Indian and Zoroastrian upbringing inform me professionally at Portland State University (PSU) where I have been for 26 years. In other words, integrity and authenticity are my moral compass and they go beyond the walls of academia.

Integrity, as I understand it, is about finding consistency between my beliefs and values and my actions. I have tried to practice what I believe by getting urban children and youth in the Portland Public School (PPS) District in touch with nature right where they live, as many poor and minority students do not have the luxury to go camping or on field trips. I have done so by nurturing and *politically* championing Learning Gardens at school sites. It is a way for me to democratize environmental education that has always appeared to me to be a luxury for those with means and power. By supporting and establishing gardens for sustainability on school sites, I have endeavored to bring life to schools and schools to life (Williams & Brown, 2011) especially for our marginalized students, many of whom are recent immigrants and/or refugees and for whom English is not a native language. This has meant using my political acumen and experience that resulted from the risk I took to run for political office city-wide, winning, and then serving as an elected official on the Portland School Board, from 2003 to 2011. In this vignette, I trace my path to political office revealing a powerful time that provided an opportunity to serve and to practice my values.

In 2002, the Portland School Board, the District administration, and the Teachers' Union were immersed in financial turmoil and communication conflict, and were at an impasse. The inability to come to a contractual agreement resulted in teachers preparing to strike. Were it not for the Portland City Council and the Mayor's office urgently intervening by providing funds to the District, the strike would have materialized—for the first time ever—in Portland. The damage in relationships and the distrust seethed deep. Despite the settlement, the horrors of low morale and name-calling, the daily barrage of negativity, and the public display of anger among Board members, Union representatives, and District administrators, threatened the vitality of the public school system with fears of exodus of the middle class that was losing confidence in PPS. "Blame game" was the norm with public and private discourse aimed at pointing fingers at leadership at all levels of the systems: the city, the district, the Board, the Union, and even the state legislature. Since I had had long-term relationships with educators and administrators at many schools, it was fairly normal for me, too, to be sucked into the norms of blaming. That was easy, as it meant I was "passing the buck" to someone else, expressing frustration, and commiserating with colleagues to find *the* culprit rather than to try to fix the systemic problems of the PPS budget crisis. In other words, I was an unwitting participant in the blame game even as I grieved for the greater good of children and respect for teachers.

Believing in democracy and social justice, my inner voice clamored for personal integrity: how to *do* what I valued to ensure that PPS stayed a robust *public* school system? As that voice called me, I testified at public meetings, participated in public marches with kids and parents to support PPS and to address the budget crisis, and even rallied on Capitol Hill in Salem to meet with our state representatives. I also provided private solace at the school level where I had relationships with educators. But, that was not enough. I was torn about simply teaching Dewey's classic *Democracy and Education,* a manifesto for a vibrant democracy linked with robust public education, and the irony of the real-life scenario of PPS' destabilization that would likely impact our communities and segregate them further. Serendipitously, I was approached by the city's civic leaders to run for Portland School Board. Suddenly, I had a choice. "If your heart is in the right place and you have good taste for it, not only will you pass muster in politics, you are destined for it," advises Vaclav Havel. I was at a crossroads: perpetuate a culture of liability and blame or take responsibility and ownership to advance the values I believed in *via* policymaking and leadership. The voice that encouraged authentic engagement with the public school system that I deeply cared about, won. And so did I, as the first Asian-American woman to be elected to the Portland School Board in 2003 and, again, unopposed for a second term in 2007. The political path of serving as an elected official was not a bed of roses; however, it showed me that with integrity I could serve, represent the marginalized, and look for systemic solutions with others. While the path traversed had many bumps and was fraught with moral dilemmas and choices, I never gave up my quest for social justice.

Although I am no longer an elected official holding political office, I feel that my life's work, also reflected in my profession, has not wavered from being political. Working with low-income communities that are often marginalized and ignored, I have cherished my long-term obligations to advance social justice and environmental health especially for the most vulnerable populations in schools. In other words, integrity brings me wholeness when I am an engaged scholar. I have absolutely no qualms meeting with the decision-makers in the District and the Board to encourage them to go beyond the normal discourse on equity and closing the achievement gap to ensure that they actually understand the need to shift paradigms toward meaningful engagement for students. I reflect on, visit, and revisit my moral actions to live by my own values with courage and to believe in collectively solving problems. As an immigrant brown woman, working with mostly white leaders in power, I do not leave the table until we find feasible solutions to the education problems we face. After all, *a la* Dewey, democracy is always in the making. Integrity demands my endurance and tenacity and that I live my values of service, social justice, and sustainability.

Chet Bowers[1]—Challenging Conceptual Orthodoxies

I arrived at UC Berkeley, intending to focus my graduate studies on European intellectual history. When I discovered that I lacked the necessary foreign languages, I found myself at the door of Frederic Lilge, refuge from Nazi Germany and professor of education, whose book, The Abuse of Learning: The Failure of the German University, was a damning assessment of the capitulation of German academics to Nazism. I was impressed by Lilge's critical approach, and that, coupled with my reading of Aldo Leopold, Rachel Carson, and the Club of Rome's Limits to Growth, led me to put together an interdisciplinary doctoral program focused on the relation of language to different constructions of reality.

It became clear to me that our current understanding of reality is shaped by taken-for-granted assumptions encoded within our linguistic systems. Metaphors and analogs settled upon by European thinkers unaware of environmental limits and captivated by the ideas of enlightenment philosophy and science, are so deeply embedded in our linguistic system as to form an unexamined curriculum, conferred on all young people who pass through our educational systems. I realized that if we are to create cultures that are ecologically and socially just, we would need to critically examine the root metaphors that kept us fastened to a worldview that was neither.

I took these ideas with me when I accepted a position in the teacher education program at the University of Oregon in 1967. I felt strongly that the conceptual orthodoxies promoted in most teacher education programs did not take account of the hidden agenda of modernity and thus inadvertently participated in serving it. I was having good success at publishing my ideas, but I had far less success convincing my colleagues to rethink the conventions of teacher education. It was not that my colleagues were any more intransigent than others. At that time, there was little engagement with environmental issues on college campuses and amongst faculty; it would sadly take many more decades before sustainability—and the intersection of social justice/ethics/economics/ecology—became an academic concern. In fact, most of my colleagues simply demonstrated the influence of the dominant paradigm on those within academic institutions.

The publication of two of my early books by Random House led to an early promotion to full professor by the time I was 35 years old. This was essential as my advocacy of unconventional ideas and my challenge of conceptual orthodoxies promoted in the teacher education program didn't always sit well with my colleagues. Not only was I challenging a number of core beliefs, but I was also pressing the discipline to move beyond the confines of specialization so that teacher education included exposure to communication theory, traditional ecological knowledge, and the burgeoning literature on sustainability. The evolution of my thinking about the cultural roots of the environmental crisis and the complicity of educational theory in validating these assumptions, led me to see the need for a full-out reform of teacher education. Needless to say, this did not boost my popularity in the department. There was a price to pay, literally; I was often passed over for merit increases, even in a year in which I had published two books.

There is great strength in conviction and though I may be accused of many failings, lack of conviction isn't one of them. The more I understood about the way values are embedded in and transmitted through language and culture and the more I understood just how damaging our modern values are to ecological and cultural systems, the stronger my convictions became regarding the need to reform not just teacher education but higher education as a whole. When the situation is as dire as I believe it is and the solutions being proffered are as superficial as I believe they are (take the uncritical embrace of computers in the classroom, for example), conviction has been my counter to the frustration and disillusionment that accompany the work of advocating for a new world view.

That doesn't mean that the work won't involve some contradictions in execution. For an academic involved in a critique of academia—indeed, for anyone involved in an effort to reform institutions from within—this is unavoidable. In my case, it meant producing books and articles, that is, high-status knowledge, about forms of knowledge (e.g. ecological intelligence, intergenerational knowledge, and traditional knowledge) that are better transmitted orally and through concrete action. It meant developing new language (e.g. the "cultural commons") and recontextualizing old language (e.g. "conservative" and "tradition") in an attempt to embed them in a culture that denies them. It meant using abstract language and theory to critique the abstraction of knowledge. The paradoxes involved in these efforts have not been lost on me but I have I been unwilling to cede clarity of thought and language to those who wrongly believe they possess them.

One more contradiction that has been a necessary part of my work has been my engagement in a global network of activists working to establish "localism" as a core dimension of sustainability. But the movement I have helped to build needs to draw on the wisdom of others, and especially for as one immersed in western traditions, it has been important for me to be exposed to the insights of non-European cultures. All along the way I have had to interrogate my own taken-for-granted assumptions; what I have learned from interaction with communities in Peru and Ecuador, in particular, has been crucial to my own efforts to become an ecologically intelligent person.

I have spent my adult life challenging conceptual orthodoxies. It has been a project that has, at times, alienated me from my closest colleagues and, indeed, heightened my own alienation from our culture. I wish I could be more sanguine that my efforts to reform higher education will yield appreciable change. But cultural shift is more likely to be the consequence of violent events than intellectual analysis. Nonetheless, there is no excuse for not exercising the power of one's convictions.

Note

1 Chet Bowers generously agreed to write this vignette, even as he was in the throes of facing terminal illness. He is no longer with us today, having passed in July 2017, shortly after writing this piece. I offer gratitude and thanks to Chet's trusted friend (and luckily for me, my neighbor and friend too), Sandra Lubarsky, for her editorial help with this vignette.

References

Bakhtin, M. M. (1990). *Art and answerability: Early philosophical essays*. (M. Holoquist, V. Liapunov, Eds., & V. Liapunov, Trans.) Texas University Press.
Blenkinsop, S., & Piersol, L. (2013). Listening to the literal: Orientations towards how nature communicates. *Phenomenology & Practice, 7*(2), 41–60.
Hampton, E. (1995). Toward a redefinition of Indian education. In M. Battiste & J. Barman (Eds.), *First Nations education in Canada: The circle unfolds* (pp. 5–46). University of British Columbia Press.
McMurtry, J. (1999). *The cancer stage of capitalism*. Pluto Press.
Palmer, P. (1998). *The courage to teach: Exploring the hidden landscape of a teacher's life*. Jossey-Bass.
Piersol, L. (2014). Listening place. *Australian Journal of Outdoor Education, 17*(2), 43–53.
Truth and Reconciliation Commission of Canada. (2015). *Truth and reconciliation commission of Canada: Calls to action*. http://trc.ca/assets/pdf/Calls_to_Action_English2.pdf
United Nations. (2008, March). *United Nations declaration on the rights of Indigenous Peoples*. http://www.un.org/esa/socdev/unpfii/documents/DRIPS_en.pdf
Williams, D. R., & Brown, J. D. (2011). *Learning gardens and sustainability education: Bringing schools to life and life to schools*. Routledge.

Part III

Learning

7

Lessons on Integrity

We live in a time of many injustices, a time in which we are tangled up in systems that are wreaking terror, pain, and havoc upon human and more-than-human lives and communities. As educators, we teach about that world. We also re-create it. In our classrooms, our research, our meals, transportation, and interpersonal relationships, we reinscribe racist, anthropocentric, colonial, capitalist, heteropatriarchal, and generally oppressive norms. We recognize—or we *need* to recognize—this. Yet, what do we do with this recognition? Knowing we are tangled up in complicities, how do we wrap our heads around what it means to live well, to live with integrity?

As I argued in the introduction, the notion that integrity is an individual virtue one can achieve when one's values align with one's actions is often a neoliberal maneuver that distracts from the real work needed for social transformation toward a world where our dreams may be more possible. The stories in the previous chapters illustrate understandings and enactments of integrity that complicate dominant assumptions about integrity. These stories do not offer one message; they come from varied positions and frameworks, some of which align more with dominant assumptions about integrity than others.

Across the stories, into the literature, and back again, I find myself holding onto three main lessons on integrity: that scale matters, to stop being one person, and to act anyway. I think of these lessons as fortune cookie notes carried in my pocket. They are reminders that I bring with me through my days. They do not tell me directly what to do, but act instead as a sounding board, as inspiration, a reminder of what I want to know about living between integrity and complicity. In this chapter, I describe these three lessons and how they are helping me re-story integrity.

Scale Matters

I tend to have two different kinds of conversations with my fellow educators about complicity and integrity. One mirrors the argument I made in the introduction: it's a distraction to focus on aligning all of your actions with all of your values, firstly because it is impossible in our world full of complicity, and secondly because this focus puts too much attention on individuals versus systems or collectives. The other involves someone explaining to me the different ways they try to "walk their talk" by changing parts of their lives to better fit their sense of what is good and right. They are both valid responses.

The trick is to understand how integrity and complicity often operate at different scales. Integrity is generally understood as individually achievable, and complicity—especially in relation to large systems of oppression—is simply not an individual project. "Integrity" is a concept that pairs an abstract value with an enacted behavior, assessing how well the abstract aligns with the actual. The focal point for comparing values to behavior is most commonly the individual. For example, a teacher (*individual*) may be said to have integrity if they *value* anti-racist education and, with that value in mind, they create and nurture a particular *behavior*, such as a school-wide restorative justice approach to disrupt their school's otherwise punitive disciplining and school-to-prison pipeline. We could say that this teacher's value of anti-racist education aligns with their behavior to implement anti-racist practices at their school, and because of that, they have integrity. However, we can also identify how, when this same teacher who values anti-racism and anti-racist schooling goes to the grocery store and buys strawberries or carrots or green beans, by virtue of their monetary support, they become complicit in a deeply racist corporate agriculture system that exploits undocumented immigrants and people of color. Likewise, when they submit their U.S. mail-in ballot for national and local elections, their vote sends a message of approval to an electoral system that has and continues to disenfranchise Black, Indigenous, and undocumented peoples on the basis of racism and xenophobia. In fact, their car, phone, the purchase of the land under their home, the clothes on their back, the energy needed to warm their home and cook food, the food that is cooked, the Tylenol they take when they get a stress headache, the very institution of K-12 schools that they work for…, these all render this teacher complicit, tangled up within, and implicated in structural forms of racism despite the incredible work they do. What we must note, however, is the difference in scale between the work that this teacher does for anti-racist education and the various ways in which they are complicit in racism. The scales are fundamentally different, and that makes all the difference.

If integrity in the face of complicity is to mean anything, it cannot mean ridding oneself of complicity writ-large, because this is outside our range/scale of possibility. Aiming for an integrity that comes once we eliminate all complicity from our lives means that we will never achieve it, that our efforts to do so might be futile. Sean Blenkinsop's vignette articulates this problem of scale as a problem of ends, suggesting that—if we judge our day-to-day actions based on something that does not yet exist, we will inevitably fall short. He writes:

> Part of the challenge of integrity rests in the question of ends; against what standard is integrity being measured. Often, for those environmentally oriented the measure is taken against an as-yet not achieved end. For example: I should not be doing X (where X involves flying to conferences, eating meat, working in an unjust/anti-ecological institutional setting, benefitting from the profligate destruction of nature, etc.), because X is not part of a Y (where Y is a way of life that is decolonized, place-based, equitable, care-based, eco-centric, etc.). And yet, for the person in question, the aimed for Y does not actually exist. Nor do the cultural boundaries, the complex set of structures, and the behavioral norms exist that might allow one to avoid doing all these problematic X acts. As a result, it is impossible for a single individual to align X and Y.

I would add to Sean's analysis that it is a problem of the *scale* of those ends against which we are attempting to measure our integrity. If we are attempting to live with integrity and measuring our goodness by whether and how we are—as Sean says—decolonized, place-based, equitable, care-based, eco-centric, always and in every single aspect of our lives, the task is not only impossible, but also often paralyzing. While we must retain a sense of responsibility for creating the world we want to live in, paralysis or defeat is not viable psychological footing from which we can rise to meet that challenge. Therefore, the scale of our goals matters not only when it comes to actually achieving them, but also in relation to our efficacy at creating larger social transformation.

Haraway's (2016) understanding of "response-ability" has been crucial in my own struggle to learn and negotiate how scale matters. Shotwell (2016) succinctly describes Haraway's response-ability as "the cultivated capacity and orientation to respond" (p. 127). When I first saw how Haraway took the word "responsibility" and turned it into "response-ability," I felt relief and insight. I went from feeling adrift in an ocean of endless responsibilities to feeling grounded within my own life. If scale matters and ridding ourselves of all complicity is outside our range/scale of possibility, how do I know what is inside my range/scale of possibility? How do I know what and how much I can do that matters? Starting with this idea of response-ability helps me answer those questions in a grounded way, a way that offers me a firmer grip on what is possible and desirable. When I ask myself what is my response-ability, I can speak from my experience. I can consider my literal ability for response, while recognizing also that my ability is not static, it can grow with cultivation. That is, in order for integrity to have meaning in a society fraught with complicity, scale matters; and Haraway's notion of response-ability gives us a frame through which to identify an appropriate scale for working through which values to align with which actions.

Response-ability goes beyond what we already know about our ability to respond and ventures out to what we might imagine and also to what we might not want to see. Haraway (2016) does not imply that we seek only what is achievable in our present-day world or that we set small, individualistic goals. There is danger in a view of integrity that limits its scope to what we can see and do, as each of us is always blind to all kinds of complicity and always living on an edge of what may be possible that we cannot yet comprehend. As Haraway (2016) explains, "Privileged positions block knowledge of the conditions of one's privilege" (p. 111). Thus, in considering our response-ability, we are also called to invoke our critical imaginations and dream up more creative, deeper levels of our ability to respond that lie beyond the horizon of what our experience to date sees and knows. This is a political process: it requires a recognition and negotiation of power. The more I can identify the power relations around and within me, the more I am able to critically imagine alternatives. Therefore, cultivating our response-ability implores us to consider not only what lies beyond the response-ability we *can* see, but also to consider what response-ability we *refuse* to see. For example, McKibben (2013) discusses a university president who ostensibly abides by the values of climate justice by driving a Prius, but refuses to consider divesting the university from fossil fuels. To live with integrity, then, requires us to interrogate our response-ability with both imagination and criticality.

While I have been writing about how integrity and complicity/contradiction often operate at different scales—integrity at the level of the individual, and complicity/contradiction at a more societal level, there are times when they *do* operate at the same scale. Specifically, there are times when it is possible, productive, and even revolutionary to align our individual personal values with our behavior, to operate at the scale of one's individual response-ability. Shotwell (2016) suggests, "Reasoning about moral matters at the scale of the individual is entirely appropriate in many, many situations.... When I decide whether it is acceptable to steal something, lie, kill someone, assist someone in suicide, and so on, in many circumstances it will be meaningful for an individual agent to make those decisions and take action appropriately" (p. 111). But, even more than this, feminists have been telling us for decades about how the personal is political, how the decisions one makes in their personal life are always resisting or reinscribing power norms. For example, Glennon Doyle (2020) describes the all-too-familiar experience that women-gendered folks—and all people to a great extent—face in going along with what is considered "right" by society's standards, even if it doesn't align with what they truly want. In her recent memoir, *Untamed,* she speaks to the power of imagining and living how we want outside of the dominant order. She uses integrity to name the process of living what is "beautiful and true" for ourselves. She writes,

> In order to get beyond our training, we need to activate our imaginations. Our minds are excuse makers; our imaginations are storytellers. So instead of asking ourselves what's right or wrong, we must ask ourselves: What is true and beautiful? (Doyle, 2020, p. 68)

An integrity that asks us to sit with our feelings, our bodies, our intuition, and to recognize and honor what we find there is within the range of a person's response-ability. It is possible, productive, and—again—even sometimes revolutionary to live it.

Continuing this conversation on what it means to find integrity at a scale where one's values can and do align with one's actions, many educators in this book share practices for how to unpack the dominant values that they learned through inculturation, and subsequently change their daily practices to align with those values.[1] Madhu asked me, and asks herself: "Are you following your bliss?" Rebecca describes the pull she feels to live "from authentic questions." David described how his experience of living with integrity includes simply asking: "How do I feel?... What am I being called toward or pushed away from, and how do I feel about it in my body?" These questions ask us to notice our feelings—in the body, in the heart. By noticing our feelings, which are perpetually marginalized in capitalist, colonial societies, we can start to identify where our desires and visions diverge from the norm. These diversions are openings, places that can transform our sense of self, purpose, possibility toward what many educators in this book call a "more authentic" self. That is, these questions about our feelings and authenticity can help us find integrity at a scale that is within our response-ability.

It is liberating and empowering to recognize and act upon our bliss, authenticity, our inner feelings of what we want, *and* it is also often hard and fraught. Doing so can mean acting outside of what is normal, expected, and rewarded. During the many years I have been working on this book, I came out as queer. At 35 years old, in a stable career, mom of two, partnered to a fantastic man, I fell madly in love with a non-binary woman.[2] It was against the script. And after much soul-searching, I chose integrity, I chose the path of honoring the wellspring of what was true and beautiful for me. My world transformed—I did not know the meaning of the word "liberated" until then. At the same time, despite my mostly supportive family and community, I struggled hard, transitioning from swimming downstream to swimming upstream in the heteronormative world we inhabit. While my experience has been challenging, I recognize that authentically living one's life can be more than simply challenging. For many queer and trans folks, the struggle to live their truth and beauty is nothing less than life threatening. Thus, I do not put this call to outwardly live one's inner integrity lightly, nor do I suggest that it is a marker of one's value or moral capacity.

Even though a greater alignment between my inner sense of what is "true and beautiful" does offer me a sense of integrity, it does not alleviate my complicity in socio-ecological injustices, even in heteropatriarchy. However, it does offer (and it can offer all of us who do this work and have these experiences) insight into how to resist oppressive forms of inculturation. When we practice resisting oppressive forms of inculturation within ourselves and our bodies, we strengthen the muscles and attunement we need to do the larger collective work of changing the societal conditions of our complicity.

Integrity necessitates that we seek to transform the conditions of our existence, not simply the alignment between our individual values and behaviors. Transforming the conditions of our existence extends beyond our individual response-ability. That is, individuals are not response-able to shift societies on their own. So, I learned that there's no way to change the injustices that plague the world I love, unless I begin to think of integrity as something that we also hold as a people, as collectives.

Stop Being One Person

Addressing the injustices that create our complicity requires that we work collectively, not individually. Kathleen Dean Moore, professor of philosophy and climate change activist, gets asked all over the country, "What can one person do?" Her compelling response is: "Stop being one person" (2016, p. 292). If we are concerned about living with integrity, it would behoove us all to do the same, to stop thinking and working as if we are solely one person.

In the United States (and other capitalist states), the state would like to convince us that our political power comes from our individual choices: submit your ballot, write a letter to your representative, and vote with your dollars because every small action adds up, right? Unfortunately not. While there is a relationship between individual ethics, actions, and social transformation, it is not as linear as most people assume. Even if we all become do-gooders, our actions would not "add up" to create the kind of socio-ecological change that would shift the conditions of our collective complicity (McKibben, 2013; Shotwell, 2016; Tsing, 2015). I used to teach a class to freshman undergraduates on trash. Many students came into the class thinking that recycling and zero-waste strategies in their homes would solve the issue of toxic run-off, poisoned wildlife, plastic islands in the ocean, and massive landfills. Through class, however, they learned that—even if *every* individual household became a "zero-waste" home, these actions would not scale up to ridding this planet of billions of tons of waste. Why? Because only 2.5% of the total waste on the planet is municipal solid waste and the rest comes from industry (Leonard, 2010, p. 186). Shotwell (2016) explains, "Ethical approaches that hold a putatively separable individual as their core unit of analysis similarly take it that individual ethical purity will be scalable, producing societal harmony. This is not the case. Rather, the terms of ethical thinking must change in relation to the scale of the ethical problem" (p. 111). Again, referring back to the section above: scale matters. When it comes to climate change, mass deforestation, forced migration, the killing of Black and Brown lives at the hands of police, industrialized agriculture, pipelines on Indigenous land (all land is Indigenous land!), and so much more, the same is true. Even when individual people change their behavior, those changes do not add up to changing the system.

Thus, my second lesson about integrity is to stop being one person and start being the interdependent beings we are. Integrity is only knowable and meaningful as it emerges in relationship to the communities, places, and time to which we belong, from which we have grown, and to which we are responsible. In short, integrity is enacted, assessed, and located within relationships to our communities. And, as each of the educators in this book reminds us, our communities are not limited to the human realm; we are always, already in relationship with myriad creatures, place communities, and life systems. To stop being one person requires attunement toward collective ethics; understanding your positionality; being responsible, accountable, and answerable; and connecting to history, seeing oneself as part of a process rather than a product. I address each of these components in the sub-sections below.

Attune Toward Collective Ethics

When I stop thinking I am one person and start practicing knowing my interdependence, I attune less to what my individual ethics are and more toward what my/our collective ethics are. Shifting from an individual unit of analysis to a collective unit of analysis makes a huge difference in what becomes possible to understand and do. For example, it is of little use to have an ethic of recycling more, but it would be of enormous use to have a collective ethic to, as some cultures have (Merchant, 2008; Graeber & Wengrow, 2021), assert that digging deep in the ground for precious minerals is a violation of our sacred Creator (Shotwell, 2016). Imagine how different the world would be if governed by cultures grounded in such ethics![3] Collective ethics, simply by the nature of being greater than the sum of their parts, have more power, greater response-ability. Response-ability is co-produced, and the power of it is increased exponentially when we think of response-ability as located not solely within the self, but within a collective. Haraway (2016) insists that response-ability is a multi-species endeavor that is always collective, describing it as "Becoming-With; Rendering-Capable" (p. 16), and "collective knowing and doing, an ecology of practices" (p. 34). When it comes to large-scale, societal issues, I need to move beyond individual frames for my ethics, out to societal, multi-species, collective frames.

All human beings, regardless of whether and how we perceive ourselves to be part of one community or another, or none at all, have collective ethics. These collective ethics provide norms and values that (often unconsciously) guide our collective behavior. Folks who are part of dominant culture(s) may not see their culture or the collective ethics that that particular culture holds. They are so ubiquitous as to remain unseen, the proverbial water in which they swim. For those who grew up in a capitalistic culture (myself included), some of our collective ethics tell us that more is better, success looks like personal gain, and happiness is an individual, unregulated freedom to pursue what we want. For many "Western" folks raised in white supremacist culture, it is essential to learn that collective ethics based on individualism, greed, and competition are *not* ubiquitous (Tuhiwai-Smith, 2012). Collective ethics based on flourishing and reciprocity in fact abound in this world, even though they are constantly under threat of erasure from genocidal, colonial forces. Luckily, as I have gotten older, and also through writing this book, I have been gifted insight into some of these much more beautiful and truly collective ethics.

Tracy Friedel and Madhu Prakash's invocations of cultural integrity and Heesoon Bai's descriptions of our "intact humanity" offer insight into what *collective* understandings and enactments of integrity might look like. Tracy's vignette highlights reciprocity and obligation to community as collective ethics that guide her work with Indigenous youth, Elders, and plants. Madhu spoke about Hindustani culture and how the ethics of caring for what is literally downstream was the (figurative) air and water she breathed in growing up, what she calls "common sense," the shared sense of common people. Similarly, Heesoon called for mutuality, solidarity, compassion, and companionship. Across all three of these examples, the collective ethics that provide grounds for a larger society with integrity are centered upon a profound sense of interdependence. That is, a collective ethics of mutuality, reciprocity, solidarity, and compassion require a deep knowing of our interdependence as ecological beings.

These stories help me shift my frame of reference from thinking of integrity as being located within individual people to integrity being located within a whole people; integrity can be something a whole culture has. As educators, we can do better at recognizing, honoring, and teaching the glorious diversity of already-existing ethics from enduring cultures all over the world that center interdependence and collectivity. Madhu, Tracy, and Heesoon's insights thus teach me to de-center both individualism and white supremacy by showing the multiplicity and abundance of collective ethics that guide whole communities through questions of how to live with integrity.

Understand Your Positionality

Some of my most transformative learning about how to stop being one person came from my visit with Ray Barnhardt. As I wrote in my portrait of Ray, he rarely would answer any of my questions about his philosophies and values and how he tried to live them. Instead, he told me that he actively avoids articulating his values and philosophies at work, preferring to facilitate or administer those conversations amongst the First Alaskan communities with whom he works. Eventually, I saw how Ray was pointing at a relational understanding of integrity: integrity can be found in the interactions (i.e. relationships) between people, places, or things. Integrity is not a destination, but an ever-changing relationship that one has to one's community.

To stop working and thinking as if we are just one person, the educators in this book say we need to know who we are, where we are from, and what our positionality is in relation to our communities. By "positionality," I mean the power we have in relation to others, power which is constituted by our intersectional locations within multiple social identities (e.g. race, class, sexuality, gender, ability, etc.). Understanding your positionality means taking a good, hard look at privilege and power. Starhawk (2011) defines privilege as "unearned social power… the power you get not from anything you've done or created, but from who you happen to be" (p. 45). Privilege is difficult and sometimes impossible to see when you have it; as I alluded to above, it is akin to (often unknowingly) swimming downstream versus having to swim upstream. Privilege is much easier to see when you do not have it. To learn about my positionality with integrity, I am in a continual process of listening and learning from/with others who have different or less privilege than me, reading about the social power structures that govern our lives, and applying that learning to the actual people and communities in my life. This process is echoed in the stories from educators in this book.

As a white settler on First Alaskan land, Ray's sense of integrity comes from knowing what power and potential he holds in relation to the communities he works with, and critically assessing how best to leverage his power in service of Indigenous autonomy in education. As I described in his portrait, this led to many different kinds of work. His goal was to essentially work himself out of a job (which he has now happily and successfully done) by using his power and privilege to set up structures that support First Alaskan students, scholars, and Elders to do the work that initially only Ray was granted the privilege to do as a white man. Ray's story shows how integrity depends upon knowing your relationship to others and shifting what you are doing as the power dynamic between you and your community shifts.

Dilafruz Williams, Tracy Friedel, Connie Russell, Richard Kahn, and Rebecca Martusewicz also exemplify how their practice of integrity is tied to understanding and leveraging their positionality. We can see this in their vignettes when they identify an aspect of their identity that compels them to use their power in a certain way. For example, Dilafruz recognizes the historical and present-day underrepresentation of women of color in high-level decision-making bodies (like school boards), and thus finds integrity in using her positionality to make the biggest influence she can in those spaces. Connie focuses her entire vignette about integrity on identifying positionality and "spending the privilege" or "leveraging" her power to make change where she can. Their stories offer helpful possibilities for how to understand one's privilege(s) and activate them with integrity.

In thinking through how I apply this lesson within my work as an educator, I find there are so many opportunities to leverage our power and positionality regularly as educators. Each time I make a decision about who to admit to the graduate program, who gets a job, what authors we will read in class, where to hold class, how to respond to harm between students, or what grade a student receives, I use my power. I often find navigating my privilege challenging and murky in some of these decisions. As just one example among many, last year I had a Black student athlete in one of my classes who went several days past the final, final "all late work is due" deadline with a 67.5%, and he needed a 70% to pass and graduate from college; mine was his final course and he took it during the final semester in which he was eligible for financial support. While I had—as many women-gendered faculty do—met with him several times one-on-one for mentoring and emotional support, extended deadlines without consequence because his family was struggling during Covid, and given him the benefit of the doubt throughout the semester, he was still missing several assignments and thus not passing. He clearly had some responsibility for the status of his grade and his missing work. And yet, I struggled knowing that grading is a generally arbitrary and punitive process that reinforces existing hierarchies (Blum, 2020), and I had the power to—past the deadline as it was—give him yet one more chance to change his grade and thereby graduate.[4] I find that I often struggle with these kinds of decisions when teaching: when do I hold fast to my boundaries (e.g. I need to receive all the final assignments by x date so that I have time to grade them before I submit grades, or there is only so much emotional work I can do for students while having enough energy to be a good human to my family), when do I make exceptions, and what is actually best and most helpful for students? In these struggles, questions of positionality arise in my reasoning: what is my positionality relative to my students? As a white, educated, cis-gendered woman with the power to assign grades, clearly I have a lot of power. Also, as a (queer) woman-gendered professor, research shows that my experience of students taking advantage of my "understanding nature" and expecting me to do a significant amount of hand-holding, emotional support, and exception-making for them is not mine alone (Lloro-Bidart & Semenko, 2017). What are the limits to my ability to leverage my power and positionality to help students navigate educational systems and structures? I am finding that answers to this question return me again to the dual notions of responsibility and response-ability.

Be Responsible, Accountable, Answerable

Questions about our positionality and privilege are closely linked to questions about how to be responsible and accountable to others. To engage with integrity means engaging with the question of how responsible, accountable, or answerable we are being to our communities and the institutions of which we are a part. As David wrote years ago (Gruenewald, 2006), "With privilege comes a *responsibility* to examine and work to transform the structures that maintain interconnected webs of privilege, oppression, violence, and multiple forms of domination and control" (p. 5). Virtually all the educators in this book talk about responsibility, accountability, or answerability as a crucial component of integrity.

My story and questions about how to leverage one's privilege from the above sub-section show that I need to remember the first lesson in this chapter: scale matters. While responsibility, accountability, and answerability are clear and crucial components of integrity, they are only so at the scales in which one is response-able (Haraway, 2016). In other words, returning to the question I ended with in the sub-section above, I need to remember that, while correcting centuries of racial violence is something I do need to confront in my individual actions, it is not something I can be individually responsible for. I can take the notion of "stop being one person" and its call to "be responsible to our communities" to an unhelpful and unhealthy place if I ignore my actual "response-ability." Shotwell (2016) helpfully clarifies, "I am interested in pursuing forms of non-innocent responsibility that do not rest on the lie that we can step outside relations of entanglement that are also always relations of suffering" (p. 121). I cannot be responsible for more than I am response-able, and no matter how much I take responsibility, I cannot step outside of my entanglement in complicity.

Even so, the educators in this book offer lessons on how to grow our response-ability along pathways that branch out from dominant understandings of who, what, and how we are response-able. Response-ability is malleable: we can become more creative, adaptive, attuned, and capacious in our response-ability. Ray

Barnhardt, Laura Piersol, Tracy Friedel, and Rebecca Martusewicz's vignettes demonstrate several possibilities for how to do so.

Ray's work exemplifies how to attune one's responsibility to a community. He does this through measuring or understanding the integrity of his work through a focus on Elders, tending to whether they show up for the work he is doing. "I know that I'm doing well through relationships: if Elders show up, we're doing something right."

Similarly, Laura and Tracy expand my sense of how and to whom we can be response-able. Tracy opens space to be responsible not to a particular entity, but to a relationship itself. Her writing describes how she cultivates her students' responsibility for maintaining the sacred bonds between plant, Elder, youth, story, and teaching. Laura's work emphasizes pushing beyond anthropocentric frames by insisting upon learning how to be response-able to the more-than-human communities of which she is a part. Her practice of integrity therefore includes explaining herself to the beings and places she has great respect for, opening herself up to listening for a response from them, and subsequently being willing to change based on what she learns. She calls this "answerability" and argues that it is deeper than responsibility because it is not simply about "accepting one's part in a scenario," but is also ultimately about a willingness to being affected and changed by another.

Of course, if integrity is partly known by being accountable, responsible, or answerable to our communities, it follows that—when and if our communities change—our ways of finding integrity change. That is, if I am judging my integrity in relation to a community of neoliberal, upper-class, white school administrators, my experience of being "responsible" to them will be starkly different than if I cultivated a community of radical teachers led by people of color who grew up in working class neighborhoods to whom I was responsible. This begs the question: to whom do you want to be responsible, accountable, or answerable? Rebecca Martusewicz's vignette illustrates how, once she ceased to quiet her inner call to center the more-than-human world in her work, this changed her community and, in turn, her sense of integrity. In no uncertain terms, she says: "My life changed. I entered a whole new set of scholarly friendships and collaborations, and community commitments. I began seeing differently, and working differently."

Not all educators will feel resonance with these various stories about responsibility, accountability, and answerability. Regardless of what feels aligned with our capacity and experience, these stories compel educators to consider several important questions. Who is in your community? Can we gauge our integrity in terms of how valued members of our community show up for the work we do and grow our response-ability through nurturing relationships with those valued community members? When I consider to whom I am responsible, can I cultivate a practice and capacity to consider, listen, and learn from the places and more-than-human beings and relationships to which I belong? Finally, how can I do more than simply accept my part, but how can I also change and respond?

Learn Your History and Connect Through Time

So far, I have explained that, to stop being one person, the educators in this book teach us to cultivate collective ethics, identify our power and positionality in relation to others, and focus upon being responsible and accountable to communities that we believe in. This last lesson about how to stop being one person adds the element of time, helping me see that integrity is a process, one that evolves and is shaped by all the histories of power, relationships, responsibilities, and ethics that are growing through time.

As interdependent beings, we are not only related to the communities and ecologies of which we are a part today, but also to those that have been and those that will be (Tsing, 2015). In my search for integrity, I am learning to "stop being one person" in part by tending to history and futurity. Alexis Pauline Gumbs, a Black feminist activist and writer, speaks of time travel (Hemphill, 2020). She says that we can and do speak with the voices of those who have come before and who will come after us, especially when we learn our histories and sit and meditate with them. In a recent interview, she explained:

> My life is not even only mine. It is an energy that has flown through for so many generations, in so many forms, and will flow through in so many forms that I can't even imagine… There's something for me in ancestral connection in particular that shows me the freedom that's available beyond the idea of myself as an individual and beyond my participation in capitalist democracy but also capitalism more broadly, in a unit called the individual—which was just created for [capitalism] to function. Not created for wellness to happen. It was not created for, you know, my family to be happy. It was created so there could be a unit through which we could be extractable. We could be understood as scarce, when we're *not*. Like, we are so infinite. We are all the time part of something infinite. So that is the freedom that's available when my life is not scarce. (9:40; 16:42)

Gumbs' words expand my sense of integrity so that my personal experience is both contextualized in a particular moment in time, and also—as she says—my personal experience of integrity is not merely my own. "My" integrity is a set of practices and possibilities that are inherited and carried on, that are "flowing through."

Ideas like "integrity" emerge from and evolve within complex histories and entanglements; integrity itself is not an isolatable, individual concept. It too evolves. The past and future shape what is "good" today. The past allows us to imagine certain futures, and what comes will allow us to imagine other futures. Richard Kahn describes this in his vignette, writing that integrity is a "process of historical improvement" whereby, "even as we appear to resolve one apparent aspect of our socio-political contradiction, its systemic nature means that it likely generates new contradictions for us to deliberate upon and change." We always exist within evolving contexts that make our experiences, decisions, and thoughts contingent upon history. What we work for, and how we work now changes the context for how we will vision and work in the future.

And so, I have come to learn that integrity is not a possession, it is a process. There is no threshold for how much integrity is "enough" to make someone or something "have integrity." Integrity is an unfolding of enactments, encounters, commitments, something that emerges in moments; it is unfinish-able, and is relational. The educators in this book highlighted a process-based orientation to integrity repeatedly. Dilafruz writes, "Integrity demands my endurance and tenacity." Heesoon suggests, "this work requires committed practice: moment-by-moment." And Rebecca says: "[Integrity is] about developing an ethics that can never be finally finished. … Staying true to those twists and turns, embracing them, even while we realize that they will shift again." Thus, to stop being one person, we have to understand how we are part of a historical trajectory, and how our integrity—individually, collectively—is not an achievable end, but it is instead a process that we partake in with past and future beings.

Knowing this, educators can ask themselves: How are we in relation to each other now and through time? What struggles did our ancestors face and what did living with integrity look like for them? How does what happened in the past broaden or narrow possibilities for how we can act with integrity today? What possibilities for integrity do I want to participate in creating for the future?

In sum, thinking and working relationally—*as more than one person*—teaches us how integrity is emergent and evolving, always in relationship to our communities, those to whom we are answerable and accountable, our cultures and collective ethics, and to our historical moment. Seeing integrity as a relational process versus a personal possession requires some work, as it is most common to understand integrity as more of a product: a characteristic we either have or not, a goal to be achieved, or a threshold to pass (e.g. we did enough things "right" to say that a person has integrity). Yet, ultimately, shifting our understanding of integrity to a process-based one is what allows us to keep going, and keep going together, rather than setting our goal at arriving.

Act Anyway

"I feel like I fail as an activist every day. But going on in spite of this despair is also part of what it means to try to live with integrity: staying true even while we fail." In this quote from her vignette, Rebecca taps into the heart of the last main lesson I learned from this research: act anyway. Action must not be forfeited on the grounds of ongoing contradictions or complicity.

Each story in this book, as well as those of countless social change activists and educators, teaches us to engage collectively in acts of resistance to socio-ecological injustices and to build resilient, nurturing communities to the best of our ability, even while we will inadvertently re-create or re-enforce oppressive norms (Brown, 2017; Dixon, 2014; Hart, McKenzie, Bai & Jickling, 2009; McKenzie, 2004; Smith, 2004; Spade, 2020). We have to be bold enough to take risks, to not be perfect, because, if we want to work to change the conditions of our complicity, there is no other option. As Chet Bowers explained in his vignette, "The work [will] involve some contradictions in execution. For an academic involved in a critique of academia—indeed, for anyone involved in an effort to reform institutions from within—this is unavoidable." Moreover, David Greenwood clarified that no matter what kind of change we are seeking—reform-based as Chet described or radical, revolutionary change—integrity is found within our acting, not in the illusory ideal of ridding ourselves of contradiction or complicity:

> We're all full of contradictions. We're not like computer programs where you can push a button and it follows a logical sequence. We're not like that. We have lots of different competing needs and desires and different ways of responding to different situations and different people, depending on what's happening at that time. Things are in flux. Like Walt Whitman says, "Do I contradict myself? Very well then, I contradict myself, I am large, I contain multitudes." That's not a cop-out from the idea of integrity. It's just a recognition that life isn't something that we play out according to our values. Our values, rather, are shaped by our interaction with life. And so, I feel like the idea of integrity is to really pay attention to

my responses to tension, to the immediate environment of my experience being in the world.

So, then, what does it mean to "act anyway," how might that look? This is a question with many valid answers and many dimensions. I will share here just a few of the key practices that I have learned through this research and that are relevant to a focus on educators. To me, acting anyway means staying with the trouble and channeling that experience of trouble into a space for learning and educating. It means prefiguring and building the communities we want in the here-and-now. And it means being strategic about how, when, and with whom to act so that we may sustain our engagement and have a greater chance at affecting change.

Learn With the Trouble

Donna Haraway's 2016 book is called *Staying with the Trouble: Making Kin in the Chthulucene*. Staying with the trouble means that, when we dig deep enough to sense our entanglement in diverse networks of interdependence, many of which we need to stay alive, and many of which involve complicity, we do not turn away. We stay there. We investigate and learn. We trouble the stories that oversimplify, embrace the entanglement, and learn to become more comfortable with discomfort. The trouble itself is educational.

Complicity and contradiction, too, are educational. Acting anyway means staying and learning with "the trouble," or the complicity. An orientation toward learning with the trouble creates growth and generativity—something we desperately need personally, societally, politically, ecologically. Alternatively, if I see making mistakes and having contradictions as a failure or take it personally, if I don't look beyond myself into the systems in which we are embedded and the systems that I (re)create, then I will become disenchanted, cynical, paralyzed, or apathetic. But, as David articulates, "The struggle is where the windows and doors open and it's the little glimpses of what you might make happen, even within the struggle, that sustain me." Dwelling within the tensions between integrity and complicity—especially if we understand how scale matters and we "stop being one person"—helps us learn and grow.

As educators, we know that struggle can be prime learning ground. In our lives, we have the dual work of being reflexively engaged in learning about our own personal "trouble," as well as facilitating that kind of reflexive learning process for and with our students. This looks like us individually staying with our own trouble and creating containers for others to do the same. Educators in this book offer lessons on how they do both.

I love Richard Kahn's framing of complicity and contradiction as the "the grounds from which we can learn to become more humane" and his assertion that integrity is "a learning exercise in how to become through the collective exercise of opposing that which prevents us." His words encourage me to understand complicity as the inevitable condition from which we grow—what he also calls "the theater of our moral progress or regress"—rather than the outcome of a poor decision on my part. Similarly, his words echo David's in describing a tension or struggle, and that tension or struggle being an essential ingredient for growth, learning, generativity—not only individually, but as collectives.

Stories about what it looks and feels like to learn with the trouble abound in these pages. On the one hand, there may be a relatively rational, reflective process whereby one strives to align a particular value with action, and then reflects on how that goes. The relative difficulty or ease affords one the opportunity to learn both about themselves and the systemic cultural, political, and economic context in which they are living. For example, if I find that it's especially hard to find and afford food that doesn't come from poisoned fields and animal prisons, then integrity comes from learning why this is so hard and acting to change the conditions that poison fields and put animals in cages. Alternatively, if it feels easy to live according to one's values, that teaches something about that person's power, privilege, the strength of their community, and/or their alignment with the dominant order. Where do we struggle to live according to our values and where do we not struggle, and what does the presence or absence of struggle teach us about ourselves, our context, and where we need to put our attention toward— as Richard said— "opposing that which prevents us" from living according to those values?

Further, learning with the trouble is sometimes less of a rational, reflexive project, and more of an emotional and embodied one. Struggle is often *felt*—it might emerge as confusion, frustration, angst, anger, sadness, or grief. These feelings themselves can be educational when we turn toward them. Feminists have been writing about the role of feeling struggle for years (Ahmed, 2017; Boler, 2004), and socio-ecological educators have similarly turned their attention more toward the role emotions play in helping educators to motivate themselves and our students as we all strive for integrity (Russell & Oakley, 2016). Similar to what I described in the Scale Matters section where I quoted David's work to simply ask "how do I feel," learning with the trouble opens the possibility of finding the trouble in our bodies and in our feelings. This can look like noticing discomfort and being curious about it: where in my body do I feel it? What is the sensation? What am I scared of? Exploring these questions is one way of learning with the trouble. And, my sense is that this learning is most powerful when—in conjunction with sitting and learning about our personal experiences—we connect our experiences to others'.

Most often, we are not alone in feeling angry, sad, or frustrated with complicity or contradiction. So, how are our feelings not only our own, but how are they part of a larger socio-cultural experience? A common exercise I do with students is have them write a *Public Narrative* (Ganz, 2009; Piersol & Timmerman, 2017). For this narrative, students begin with their personal experiences and feelings in a "story of self:" what is a difficult experience or choice I have had to make? What is one issue in my experience that makes me uncomfortable, angry, or sad? Then, the second part of the narrative is a "story of us:" how is my experience not only my own? Who else shares this experience and what unites those of us who do? Finally, the last section is a "story of now:" what actions can we take together in this moment to address our collective experiences? All of us—including myself—write these narratives and share them aloud with one another. This allows us to feel and learn from our individual "trouble," as well as witness and learn how that trouble is collective.

When we hold space for students to learn through the trouble, Madhu and Rebecca explain that part of the role educators play is to help students identify the trouble in the first place. Students may not know or have language to explain the social, political, cultural, and economic systems that structure our collective lives. Madhu and Rebecca also point out that, once they do the work to help students know "the trouble," the second half of their job is to allow students to stay with it: feel, reckon, negotiate, and possibly transform it. Connie and Heesoon echoed this experience, but added an explanation of how working with students is reciprocal and goes both ways. For example, Connie writes that, "identifying… contradictions is integral to my pedagogy, and I try to model being grateful rather than defensive when students bring them to my attention."

Educational spaces—whether in school classrooms or community forums—are spaces where our primary purpose is to learn from and with each other. Learning with the trouble requires outside perspective and collective dialogue, both of which are within our power to facilitate as educators. Learning with the trouble asks educators: how can you create space for your own uncovering of the trouble, for a group of learners to uncover theirs, and for a vulnerable, collaborative dialogue that enables critical connection and support?

Prefigure Our Communities

Prefiguration is a term that emerged from anti-oppressive and anti-establishment activist communities (Dixon, 2014; Shotwell, 2016). By definition, these communities are dedicated to social transformation. Typically, there are two kinds of goals in activist communities of this sort: 1) resist and fight the dominant power structures and 2) rebuild something better. Prefiguration, or what is also often called "prefigurative politics," refers to the art of practicing, experimenting with, and attempting to implement that something better in the here and now. That is, instead of only fighting against the power structures that are creating injustice and exploitation, our communities can also engage in that fight in a way that models the kinds of relationships and structures we envision as alternatives (Boggs, 2012). Harsha Walia's (2013) definition reiterates this point: "[prefiguration is] the notion that our organizing reflects the society we wish to live in—that the methods we practice, institutions we create, and relationships we facilitate within our movements and communities align with our ideals" (p. 11).

To be clear, prefigurative praxis did not emerge as a "finding" from my research for this book. Rather, it is an idea and practice that I learned about during the analysis and chose to bring into the conversation because of its relevance. Having said that, even though educators' stories in this book do not mention prefigurative praxis by name, some of the portraits and vignettes demonstrate what it can look like in practice.

Chris Dixon's (2014) extensive research on activist communities found four common forms of prefigurative praxis, each of which are mirrored in the varied understandings and practices of integrity that have been storied within this book. Dixon explains these four types of prefigurative activities as: 1) "practicing countercultural lifestyles that in some way point toward a better society" (e.g. vegetarianism, nonmonogamy, etc.); 2) "building and running counter-institutions, such as food co-ops, free community health clinics, and land trusts;" 3) horizonal forms of community organizing: "bringing people together in ways that build their collective power;" and 4) "creating and practicing more egalitarian modes of interacting within movement contexts" (e.g. consensus decision-making, anti-oppression practices) (p. 85). Across each of these types of prefigurative praxis is a collective commitment to tend to both the means and the ends of our work. In other words, rather than using the status quo structures, lifestyles, or relationships in our work to try and build a liberatory and ecologically flourishing society, we will practice putting into place new structures, lifestyles, or relationships that we hope may be possible in that liberatory and flourishing world.

Getting into specifics of what prefiguration looks like, an example within an organizing context could play out as follows: if our labor union has a vision of a world where we prioritize fun as much as (or more) than paid labor, then when we hold our meetings and plan how to make demands for more paid time off, we ensure that those meetings themselves prioritize fun and pleasure amongst ourselves as much as they prioritize strategizing, planning, and delegating. In an educational context, if we have a vision of a world where the natural world is a teacher, then this means not only having our students read, discuss, and write about why our schooling is so anthropocentric, but also practicing holding class outside regularly and practicing learning from the more-than-human worlds in our communities. Laura Piersol, Sean Blenkinsop, and Tracy Friedel aptly demonstrated this kind of prefigurative praxis in their vignettes. Or, if our visions and values include non-hierarchal or anti-authoritarian social structures, then we not only teach our students about cooperation, collaboration, and horizonal forms of power, but maybe we experiment with ungrading in the classroom (a practice of qualitative, self, and peer assessment that avoids numerical, hierarchical grading; see Blum, 2020 and Stommel, 2020). There are many options for prefigurative praxis in an educational context. The key is that we imagine the world as though it might be otherwise (Greene, 2007), and work to simultaneously create that world within our sphere of influence, *and* make that world possible at a much larger societal scale.

Prefiguration is not easy work; it is fraught with contradiction and tension because the larger structures and cultures of our lives do not support or have not prepared us for the kinds of people we want to be. Additionally, Dixon (2014) alerts readers that some common dangers of prefigurative praxis are that it becomes too insular and self-absorbed or too rigid and self-righteous. In a similar way to how integrity can be conflated with purity, innocence, or righteousness, so can prefigurative praxis ("if you don't do x, y, z in your classroom you are not right or good enough"). Finally, similar to integrity feeling like a product rather than a process, prefigurative praxis can also feel like a checklist rather than an experiment (e.g. "if I attend regular workshops on how to be an anti-racist educator, and I make sure to start all of my classes with a check-in, then I've done it!"). The lesson here is to remember that focusing solely on how we do things will not change the larger social context. "Prefigurative politics importantly links means and ends, but we can sometimes get transfixed on our means *as* ends" (Dixon, 2014, p. 101). As with so many parts of life, prefiguring our communities is most effective in a "both/and" frame where we work both on the means (creating a new way of being together/prefiguration), and the ends (resisting and changing what does not serve life/social transformation).

Prefigurative praxis challenges me as an educator to ask myself: what are my wildest dreams and visions for my students, our learning space, and our practice of learning? What are their dreams for their own learning? And, what can I do today or this week to try out our collective visions in the here-and-now, rather than waiting for the larger structure to change? Simultaneously, what can we do to change that larger structure so that all of us might be able to more easily live our dreams?

Strategize

I have been on a huge learning journey in relation to strategy in recent years. In part, this was spurred on by my observations that environmental education was largely not reaching its goals. Environmental educators wanted to end environmental destruction and environmental injustice, so we taught about what was happening, why, how to respond, and aimed to do so in ways that fostered connections between students and the more-than-human world. Yet, despite our efforts, growing research in the field, and wider societal acceptance of environmental and sustainability movements, climate change, mass extinction, and myriad other problems continue to proliferate. Many environmental educators have robust explanations for why. I began to seek answers to my own questions of "why" by looking to social movement history. How did people who have been part of making large scale social change in the past do it? What does it take to make large-scale social change? What would it take to actually change the conditions of our complicity? This history reveals many things, several of which I've already written about in the book, such as how scale matters and the need to act relationally with responsibility and accountability. One thing I had not seen in environmental education conversations, however, was the need to *strategize*.

Strategy means understanding one's personal and collective power and using that power to leverage for change in ways that are most likely to result in the most substantial, lasting changes. There are so many actions each of us could take; which are most strategic? I see so many of those interested in social change get wrapped up and stymied at the level of "I have to make a change! I have to *do* something. I have to take action." Yet, most educators—most people in general—are not well versed in political strategy. What kinds of actions are most strategic? To answer this question, you have to learn a lot about your power and privilege, as I described in the section above. You also have to—and again, here is where even more people get stuck—stop thinking of yourself only as one person. Inevitably, we will *always* have more power if we act as collectives of people rather than as individuals. It is always more strategic to organize with others in a similar position to make a collective demand. Although the history books love to idolize individual social change leaders—Martin Luther King, Jr., Angela Davis, Malcolm X, Cesar Chavez, Martha P. Johnson—social transformation happens when a multitude of collectives strategically pressure decision makers and people in positions of power over an extended period of time (Chenoweth, 2021; Engler & Engler, 2016; Garza, 2020; Piven, 2006).

Several of the educators in this book discuss strategy, however most do so from the vantage point of their individual decisions. Both Connie Russell and Dilafruz Williams spoke directly to making strategic decisions about where to put their energy, and where not to put it. In particular, Connie's vignette pointed toward how acting strategically is not only a matter of what one *does*, but also what one *refuses* to do: "I thus tried to be strategic, putting some tasks on the back burner, refusing to do others altogether, and prioritizing those I thought would best achieve my goals." These kinds of strategic decisions make material differences in our lives and in the lives of others. Yet, Connie also recognized the limitations of working alone within an institution: "Even so, I worried I was nonetheless consenting to an audit culture that I find counterproductive. Audre Lorde's words about the master's tools never dismantling the master's house echoed in my ears."

While several education scholars agree that collective, strategic action in the face of contradiction is key (Boggs, 2012; Hart, McKenzie, Bai, & Jickling, 2009; Fawcett, 2000; McKenzie, 2004; McKibben, 2013; Smith, 2004), examples from educators' day to day lives were harder to come by. Few discussed collective strategy, that is, strategizing from the position of interdependence (Piven, 2006). This is most certainly a limitation of my initial framing of the prompts I gave them. Yet, it is also a broader trend in our individualistic society.

As greenhouse gasses continue to be released into the atmosphere at increasing levels, forests are burned to make way for industrial agriculture, and world politics veer deeper into (eco)fascism (Malm & the Zetkin Collective, 2021), I believe that environmental educators need to get more strategic. If we see our field as one that is an advocacy, activist, or political field, then it is crucial to understand and apply the strategies identified by social transformation researchers on how social transformation actually happens. We are at a moment where it is imperative for us to ask: what political and economic powers are at work that are creating the conditions of such ecological and social injustice? What can social movement and social transformation experts teach us about how to change those conditions? As educators, what power do we have in this political landscape, and what power do we not have? How have educators used their power historically to be part of social transformation, and how might we use our power today to be most effective? Because I find this need to work on strategy imperative, I return to it in the final chapter.

Conclusion

The thing is: I am complicit. In ways that I am terrified and embarrassed to admit, in ways that I do not even understand. The scale of those complicities is so vast. Yet, I am deeply committed to changing the conditions of our collective (yet differentiated) complicity. I will not let stories of hypocrisy and contradiction trick me into thinking that I am personally responsible for eliminating complicity. I will remember that scale matters, that I can and will cultivate my response-ability. I will do so with others. We will question and reflect upon our positionality and how that influences our responsibility. We will stop seeing ourselves as individuals, knowing interdependence with more-than-human beings here and now, and into the past and future. When we feel messy and overwhelmed, we will stay with that trouble by listening and learning. We will use our listening and learning to grow our capacity to respond to places we had not before known. Our capacity to respond will be channeled strategically, prefiguratively. More will become possible then. And we will turn our hearts and minds toward those possibilities, cycling again back to more interdependence, more learning, more intentional actions, more integrity.

Notes

1. While participants' views expressed here may strictly be their understandings, they are also inevitably affected by the ways in which I framed my questions during interviews and when I solicited vignettes, which at times had this individualized frame embedded within them.
2. There are no appropriate words in the English language that feel like a good fit for my partner's gender.
3. It does not take much to imagine how different things would be: some history lessons and observation of how Indigenous communities are and have been living for time immemorial. See Graeber & Wenrow's 2021 Dawn of Everything book.

4 To satisfy the reader's curiosity, what I ended up doing was reach out to give this student yet one more opportunity to submit a missing assignment worth a substantial part of the grade. Once he did, his grade was raised to passing and he happily graduated.

References

Ahmed, S. (2017). *Living a feminist life*. Duke University Press.

Bakhtin, M. M. (1990). *Art and answerability: Early philosophical essays*. (M. Holoquist, V. Liapunov, Eds., & V. Liapunov, Trans.). Texas University Press.

Blum, S. D. (Ed.) (2020). *Ungrading: Why rating students undermines learning (and what to do instead)*. West Virginia University Press.

Boggs, G. L. (2012). *The next American revolution: Sustainable activism for the twenty-first century*. University of California Press.

Boler, M. (2004). *Feeling power: Emotions and education*. Taylor & Francis.

Brown, A. M. (2017). *Emergent strategy: Shaping change, changing worlds*. AK Press.

Brown, W. (2015). *Undoing the demos: Neoliberalism's stealth revolution*. Zone Books.

Chang, D. (2016). The sticky side of hypocrisy: Environmental activism in an oil-drenched world. *Philosophical Inquiry in Education, 23*(2), 200–202.

Chenoweth, E. (2021). *Civil resistance: What everyone needs to know*. Oxford University Press.

Dixon, C. (2014). *Another politics: Talking across today's transformative movements*. University of California Press.

Doyle, G. (2020). *Untamed*. The Dial Press.

Engler, M., & Engler, P. (2016). *This is an uprising: How nonviolent revolt is shaping the twenty-first century*. Nation Books.

Fawcett, L. (2000). Ethical imagining: Ecofeminist possibilities and environmental learning. *Canadian Journal of Environmental Education, 5*, 134–149.

Ganz, M. (2009). What is public narrative: Self, us & now [public narrative worksheet]. Working paper. Digital Access to Scholarship at Harvard. https://dash.harvard.edu/handle/1/30760283

Garza, A. (2020). *The purpose of power: How we come together when we fall apart*. One World.

Graeber, D., & Wengrow, D. (2021). *The dawn of everything: A new history of humanity*. Farrar, Strauss and Giroux; Macmillan.

Greene, M. (2004, February). *Imagination, oppression and culture/creating authentic openings* [conference presentation]. Interrupting Oppression and Sustaining Justice Conference, New York, NY, United States. https://maxinegreene.org/uploads/library/imagination_oc.pdf

Gruenewald, D. A. (2006). Resistance, reinhabitation, and regime change. *Journal of Research in Rural Education, 21*(9), 1–7. http://www.umaine.edu/jrre/21-9.pdf

Haraway, D. (2016). *Staying with the trouble: Making kin in the Chthulucene*. Duke University Press.

Hart, P., McKenzie, M., Bai, H., & Jickling, B. (Eds.) (2009). *Fields of green: Restorying culture, environment, and education*. New York, NY: Hampton Press.

Hemphill, P. (Host). (2020, October, 19). Remembering with Alexis Pauline Gumbs (No. 7) [Audio podcast episode]. In *Finding our way*. https://findingourwaypod.buzzsprout.com/1108100/5955562-ep-7-remembering-with-alexis-pauline-gumbs

Leonard, A. (2010). *The story of stuff: The impact of overconsumption on the planet, our communities, and our health–and how we can make it better*. Free Press.

Lloro-Bidart, T., & Semenko, K. (2017). Toward a feminist ethic of self-care for environmental educators. *Environmental Education Research, 48*(1), 18–25. https://doi.org/10.1080/00958964.2016.1249324

Malm, A., & the Zetkin Collective. (2021). *White skin, black fuel: On the danger of fossil fascism*. Verso.

McKenzie, M. (2004). The "willful contradiction" of poststructural socio-ecological education. *Canadian Journal of Environmental Education, 9*, 177–190.

McKibben, B. (2013, March/April). A moral atmosphere: Hypocrisy redefined for the age of warming. *Orion, 32*(2), 15–16.

Merchant, C. (2008). *Radical ecology: The search for a livable world* (2nd ed.). Routledge.

Moore, K. D. (2016). *Great tide rising: Towards clarity and moral courage in a time of planetary change*. Counterpoint.

Palmer, P. (1998). *The courage to teach: Exploring the inner landscape of a teacher's life*. Jossey-Bass.

Piersol, L., & Timmerman, N. (2017). Reimagining environmental education within academia: Storytelling and dialogue as lived ecofeminist politics. *Journal of Environmental Education, 48*(1), 10–17.

Piven, F. F. (2006). *Challenging authority: How ordinary people change America*. Rowman & Littlefield Publishers.

Russell, C., & Oakley, J. (2016). Editorial: Engaging the emotional dimensions of environmental education. *Canadian Journal of Environmental Education, 21*, 13–22. https://cjee.lakeheadu.ca/article/view/1528

Shotwell, A. (2016). *Against purity: Living ethically in compromised times*. University of Minnesota Press.

Smith, A. (2016). Heteropatriarchy and the three pillars of white supremacy: Rethinking women of color organizing. In INCITE! Women of Color Against Violence (Eds.), *Color of Violence: The INCITE! Anthology* (pp. 66–73). Duke University Press. https://doi.org/10.1215/9780822373445-007

Spade, D. (2020). *Mutual aid: Building solidarity during this crisis (and the next)*. Verso.

Stommel, J. (2020, February 06). Ungrading: An FAQ. https://www.jessestommel.com/ungrading-an-faq/

Tsing, A. L. (2015). *The mushroom at the end of the world: On the possibility of life in capitalist ruins*. Princeton University Press.

Tuck, E., & Yang, K. W. (2012). Decolonization is not a metaphor. *Decolonization: Indigeneity, Education & Society, 1*(1), 1–40.

Tuhiwai-Smith, L. (2012). *Decolonizing methodologies: Research and Indigenous peoples* (2nd Ed.) Zed Books.

Walia, H. (2013). *Undoing border imperialism*. AK Press.

8

So Much Is Possible

Ironically, it turns out that this concept of integrity is full of contradiction. Integrity is both a virtue that a person can have, and integrity is a process, never static, always an enactment, but never possessed. Integrity is both sought and found within the individual self, and integrity is sought and found with communities. Integrity is both about eliminating contradiction, and integrity is about not getting hung up on contradiction, but acting well in the world we encounter. What matters here is the both/and framing. None of these statements is helpful without its counterpart. Alone, they are dangerously simplistic. Together, they begin to get at the tensions and complexity that make integrity useful.

The educators' stories of integrity and complicity in this book encompass more topics than I can wrap my mind around in any given moment. They ask us to seek integration with/in our inner and outer selves. Thrive amidst paradox. Listen and learn from nature. Tend the traditional relationships between people and land. Commit to and care for each other. Be answerable. Endure. Use our power. Resist, refuse, and stop apologizing. Rejoice in compassion and love. Find our bliss. Do it together.

Against the backdrop of such rich, dynamic lessons, when I face my complicity now, I turn away from stories of hypocrisy and turn toward possibility. The educators in this book, along with the colleagues and friends who have accompanied me on this inquiry over the last many years, have taught me the power of focusing upon possibility, of knowing and demanding and acting in ways that show how complicity is not a dead end. In the act of turning toward what is possible, we can in fact *increase* what is possible. Through our stories, actions, and attention, we can cultivate and nurture response-ability within ourselves and our communities (Brown, 2017; Haraway, 2016).

For those of us concerned with dismantling systems of oppression, as long as we are committed to critically revisiting our response-ability, we would do well to drop an overt concern with hypocrisy. David Chang (2016) reminds us, "When surrounding conditions severely limit a person's ability to align actions with values, hypocrisy ceases to be a relevant criticism" (p. 201). Narratives of hypocrisy further the illusion that scale does not matter, that our individual decisions are of the utmost importance, and that we cannot do anything right until we escape the hypocrisy of what it means to be alive in a capitalist, colonial culture. But actually, I am learning that we can do so, so many things right.

I started the research for this book feeling agitated, stuck, and like I could turn nowhere without being or doing *wrong*. I have a deep undercurrent to my personality that seeks out and finds my own self-worth in knowing and acting on what is "right." But as I mature, as I have grown my community, and as I dove into this research, I am learning from wise ones to say: there is *no* single right way. There is only creativity, curiosity, collaboration, persistence, experimentation, learning, and staying with the trouble. Rightness is not a formula or an innocence, rightness is courage and beauty and a feeling in our bodies. There are so many possibilities for you, for us. What will we create?

So, instead of mulling over hypocrisy, I encourage the part of me that so badly yearns to be right to turn toward possibility, toward abundance, toward strategy. In an interview about working collaboratively across borders to face the climate crisis, Harsha Walia asks, what happens if we resist the dominant scarcity logic in our capitalist society and emphasize abundance instead—how we have so much space, resource, and strength in our history (Geiger & Weiland, 2019)? What happens if I invoke my imagination? What happens if, as Shotwell (2016) says, I give myself the Zapatismo possibility of "many yesses" (p. 19)? Or, as Sean wrote in his vignette, we "find a way to live in this space between the order and the chaos," and we find our integrity within the "range of possibilities that are both allowable and that we can imagine?"

In the introduction, I wrote: *we need the practice of envisioning the world in which we want to live and working to bring that world into existence.* To do so, we need permission to unleash our most wild and visionary imaginations. A whole wild field, rich with possibility, lies before us. If we emphasize hypocrisy, complicity, or contradiction, we fear for the damage we might do by stepping in any direction. If we emphasize possibility, abundance, and strategy, we feed our creativity as we walk through the multitude of decisions in our lives. Our passage through the field is what allows us to grow, to pick up seeds and pollens, participating in the vast and complex unfolding of our collective lives. Run through the field!

I worried

I worried a lot. Will the garden grow, will the rivers flow in the right direction, with the earth turn as it was taught, and if not how shall I correct it?

Was I right, was I wrong, will I be forgiven, can I do better?

Will I ever be able to sing, even the sparrows can do it and I am, well, hopeless.

Is my eyesight fading or am I just imagining it, am I going to get rheumatism, lockjaw, dementia?

Finally I saw that worrying had come to nothing. And gave it up. And took my old body and went out into the morning, and sang.

- Mary Oliver (2010, p. 39)

Possibilities Beyond This Book

Each step reveals a new vista, and so it is that after the many steps it took to finish this project, I have new sights in my eyes. The choices I made in the framing of the question at the heart of this book, the way I gathered stories for it, and the lessons I have knitted together all reveal yet more possibilities for future inquiry.

Methodologically, I found the use of portraiture rewarding. I love stories, I love the complicated framing of searching for goodness and writing a portrait that is both scholarly and literary. Portraiture offered me a unique format through which to grapple with my positionality and norms through its non-normative approach to validity. I played with switching between first and third person voices to signal moments of differentiation or critical questioning between myself and participants. Additionally, portraiture lends itself to the inclusion of more-than-human voices as actual participants. While I did not delve deeply into this possibility within this research project, I remain compelled and intrigued by it. Since completing my research, there is an edited book devoted to this very topic titled *Ecoportraiture in Education: Learning and Storying with the More-Than-Human* (Blenkinsop, et al., 2022) in which I contributed a chapter on how the research in this book might have ventured into what the editors call "ecoportraiture" (Timmerman, 2022).

As with any research project, the scope and diversity of my participants was limited, and I can easily identify many possibilities for their expansion. The addition of the nine vignettes addressed this limitation to a degree, yet it would also be wonderful to read stories from community-based educators, K-12 educators, and/or activist educators. Stemming from my experience with this project, I realized that a portrait could be collective, representing the voices of a group, rather than an individual. This possibility for a collective portrait has been explored by some researchers in the past (Davis, et al., 1993; Pickeral, et al., 2003). More recently, I have chosen to experiment with writing portraits of groups in my current research on historical cases of disruptive faculty activism (Timmerman, 2021).

The question I asked David on the top of Kamiak Butte: *what is the civil disobedience of an environmental educator,* planted a seed for the new questions I find myself asking today. Toward the end of completing my dissertation (the core of the research for this book), I began to engage more deeply in community organizing. Starting with a struggle to prevent the demolition of family housing at my graduate university, to non-tenure track faculty labor organizing once I started a job, to mutual aid with undocumented communities in Northern Arizona, I have been learning a lot about collaborative resistance and community care. Through this work, I realized how little most people know about how to create lasting and substantive social transformation. While it is certainly a mystery in some ways, there is a whole field of social movement and social transformation studies, and moreover there are scores of grassroots activists who hold an intergenerational wealth of knowledge and practice on the topic. Merging my questions about how to live a good and meaningful life with my practice of social transformation, I started to ask questions about how postsecondary faculty could engage in activist work beyond a radical syllabus or community-based research project.

Thus, the research in this book opens several possibilities for new and different research. For me, the questions I am pursuing now ask how postsecondary educators have historically engaged in collective, disruptive forms of activism for social movements (Timmerman, 2021). The analysis I did for the "Lessons on Integrity" chapter shows that educators know that acting strategically is important, yet their options for doing so are primarily informed by dominant political norms. From years of teaching strategic action in social movements, my sense is that most of us are limited in our strategic options by lack of knowledge and vision, more than by a lack of possibility. Therefore, other questions to ask are: how does political strategy work, both on a large societal scale, as well as within in educational institutions? How can educators invested in social transformation learn from the histories and present-day movements about how to do it? What diverse options do educators have for working collaboratively and strategically for social transformation with students, staff, and other faculty?

Ask the Questions

I wonder about this book I have written and what it can do, what its purpose is. I initially wrote that I am interested in re-storying integrity. "What a gargantuan and ridiculous task," my doubts quip. It is true that this work to write new and different stories about integrity is a small drop in a bucket, and it is also true that—while I have been contending with these questions for many years now—I am underequipped and ignorant to take on the task. Yet, this book remains a certain kind of offering, one that I hope does give some new stories and new direction for folks who feel caught in complicity and who strive to live with integrity.

What I know is that I still get stuck in questioning how to live well in a time that feels so oppressive, that feels like so many things are wrong. How can I do something right when so many things—including things that make me who I am, the things that make me tick, think, feel, and the things that support my day-to-day living! —are wrong? From having taught for so many years now, I know that I am not the only one who asks this question. And this question can come from so many places: it can come from despair, pity, abstraction and distancing, shame, avoidance, rationalization, a religious call to perfectionism. We can—and should—critically question where the question comes from. And I do find critiques in the question. But I cannot dismiss it, even though the critiques are valid. Even though the question of "how can I live well in a time where I replicate injustice" is individualistic, even though it's indicative of neoliberal politics, even though it implies an unachievable answer, it is an important question. It can also come from grief, from response-ability, from accountability, from humility! Our hearts implore us.

What I have to offer is this: ask your questions about how to be good when you are complicit in so many evils. Ask the question again and again. But, as you do so, do not delude yourself into thinking that the answer to this question 1) exists, or 2) will solve your dilemma. The answer to this question comes in the asking and the doing, the question and the answer are both processes of living. And there is no such thing as "your dilemma" because there is only "our dilemma." Furthermore, the dilemma we face is not just a dilemma of being complicit in systems of oppression in the 21st century. The dilemma we face is a dilemma of any person who finds themself living in a society or community that is in need of change.

So, ask your questions over and over, ask them as a process. Approach your questions with both skepticism and criticality, and also approach them with compassion and nurturance. If you want to wrestle with the concepts of integrity and complicity in your life, get used to thinking in terms of "both/and." Gather your wits: dive into who you are, know yourself, know your power, know who you are in relation to your people, your land, and your ecologies. And, with them, engage in dialogue. Ask your people, your land, and your ecologies how you can be responsible and answerable to them. Be ready to explain yourself to them, come up short handed, and need to change yourself or your actions. And, as you engage in this dialogue, listen to the conversation as a whole. Work toward articulating not only your own understanding of what is good and what it means to live well, but work toward articulating what it means to your people, your land, and your ecologies to be good and to live well. Remember that you will not arrive at a final answer. Your answers are always part of a conversation amongst beings that are growing, evolving, and changing, and thus your conversation will grow, evolve, and change as well. Be patient, persevere, stay curious. Even though you will not have final, unchangeable answers, your conversation will come to strong footholds, to ideas and convictions that you find to be true and beautiful and good. When you find what is true and beautiful, especially if you have done so through critically engaging in both/and inquiry and within community, try it. Try to be true and beautiful. You will fail. Try anyway. Apologize. Try again. Create spaces where you can try with others and you will make each other stronger. Educate each other, stay with the trouble.

Ask your questions about how to be good, how to do good, in a world where suffering is sown within, through, and by us. These are actually damn good questions. They are especially good questions if you use them to open up possibility. Do not use these questions to talk about something as trite as hypocrisy. Use them to vision, to dream, to empower, to activate, to gather, and to inspire.

References

Blenkinsop, S., Fettes, M., & Piersol, L. (Eds.) (2022). *Ecoportraiture in education: Learning and storying with the more-than-human.* Peter Lang.
Brown, A. M. (2017). *Emergent strategy: Shaping change, changing worlds.* AK Press.
Chang, D. (2016). The sticky side of hypocrisy: Environmental activism in an oil-drenched world. *Philosophical Inquiry in Education, 23*(2), 200–202.
Geiger, L., & Weiland, A. (2019, October 18). *Harsha Walia Interview* [video]. Berliner Gazette. Vimeo. https://vimeo.com/367214798
Haraway, D. (2016). *Staying with the trouble: Making kin in the Chthulucene.* Duke University Press.
Oliver, M. (2010). *Swan: Poems and prose poems.* Beacon Press.
Shotwell, A. (2016). *Against purity: Living ethically in compromised times.* University of Minnesota Press.
Timmerman, N. (2021, December 6–10). *Portraits of disruptive faculty activism in 20th Century social movements* [conference presentation]. Society for Research into Higher Education 2021 Annual Conference, London, UK.
Timmerman, N. (2022). Relationship, complexity, and co-creation in portraiture research. In S. Blenkinsop, M. Fettes, & L. Piersol (Eds.), *Ecoportraiture in education: Learning and storying with the more-than-human,* 23–46. Peter Lang.

List of Index Terms

A

absolutism 123-124
abundance 151, 172-173
accountability 12, 18, 19, 97, 101, 131, 150, 154-156, 158
action alignment 9, 11, 110, 114, 121-123, 131, 144-147, 170
   acting anyway 7, 158-166
   taking action 49, 75, 149
activism, activists 72, 121, 123, 126, 133, 135, 158, 162, 166, 174
administration, (educational) 94-97, 99, 110-114, 121-123, 136
advocacy, advocates 94, 108, 114, 123, 138-139
aesthetics 16-17, 21-23, 27-28
affection 63, 73, 79, 83
agriculture *see* farming
Ahmed, Sara 123, 161

Alaska Rural Systemic Initiative (AKRSI) 95-96, 101
Alaska Cultural Standards 110, 112
Alaska Federation of Natives 92, 95, 115
alignment 11, 13, 85, 94, 148, 160
altruism 109
ambiguity 8, 17-19, 23-26
ancestors 118, 156-157
anger 4, 128-129, 136, 160-161
angst 126, 160-161
anonymity (in research) 18, 24
answerability 131-132, 154-157
anti-racism 65-66, 105, 126, 144-145
apologizing 133
art (in research) 16-17, 20-23, 27-28
Assembly Line, B. Traven 64
attunement 148, 150, 154-155
authenticity 8, 23-24, 57, 59, 82-84, 133, 136, 147-148
autonomy 54, 77
awareness 25, 77-78, 86, 106, 131

B

Bai, Heesoon 128-130, 151, 157, 161
balance 42, 57, 123
Barnhardt, Ray 21-22, 30, 89-116, 151-152, 155
beauty 75-76, 78-79, 85, 147-148, 170, 174
behavioral change 42, 127, 134, 144, 147-150
being outside 40, 43-44, 47, 126-128, 130-132
belonging 66, 106, 119, 150, 156
Berry, Wendell 37, 67, 72, 76-78, 109
blaming, blame game 4-5, 78, 136
Blenkinsop, Sean xiv, 126-128, 145, 163, 170
bliss 82-84, 86, 147-148
both/and 44, 114, 125, 163-164, 169, 174
Bowers, Chet 99, 137-140, 158
burnout 40, 122

C

Camus, Albert 127-128
capitalism 4-5, 12, 36-37, 72, 98, 102, 143, 148-149, 151, 156, 170
   anti-capitalism 71, 90
care 7, 18-19, 127, 129-130, 132-133, 135, 145, 172
   ethics of care 18-19
   self-care 123
chaos 128, 170
civil disobedience 49-50, 172
co-created knowledge 20-24, 101
cohesion (in research) 27-28
collectivity 85, 102, 108, 123, 148, 157, 161, 165, 172
   collective ethics 150-151

colonialism, colonization 5, 36-37, 65-66, 101, 105, 118, 120
   anti-colonial *see* decolonization
coming out 148
commitment 54, 75, 92, 108, 120, 133, 137, 139, 157, 162
common sense 66-69, 151
community organizing 162-166, 172
companionship 130, 151
compassion 129-130, 134-135, 151
competition 101, 129-130, 151
complexity 5-6, 44, 127, 169
   in research 15, 17-20, 24-25
complicity
   explanations of 4-6, 9-11, 77-78, 108, 129, 144-148, 158-161, 169-170
   personal experience with 3, 42, 52-53, 114, 127, 166
   research on 6-9, 12-13
   see also contradiction(s)
conformity 36, 42, 51, 60, 103-105
conspiring 46, 60
contradiction(s) 4-5, 9, 12, 48, 52-53, 77-80, 114, 121-122, 124-127, 157-161, 169
   in research 29
   see also complicity
conviction 139
corporation greed 35-36
courage 55, 81-82, 123, 134, 137, 170
critical theory 46-47, 125
cross to bear 77-80
Cuernavaca, MX 72, 74
cultural awareness 105-106
cultural colonization 69-70, 92 *see also* colonialism, colonization
cultural reproduction *see* living as learning
cultural transmission *see* living as learning

culturally relevant education 90, 92, 95, 100-101, 110, *see also* Indigenous education
cynicism 159

D

de Beauvoir, Simone 127
decolonization 44, 71, 90
democracy 70, 135-137
Deschooling Society 71
detoxification 129
development, "undeveloped" 65-66, 70-72, 77, 89-90, 125
dialectic 125
discomfort 159-161
distance learning 102-108
diversity 104, 111-112, 151
Dixon, Chris 162-163
domestication (of the Ivory Tower) 102-103, 105
Doyle, Glennon 147

E

ecoportraiture 17, 172
ecological education *see* environmental education
ecological literacy 72, 77
ego, egocentrism 56, 75, 129-130
Elders, Elder participation 77, 90, 96, 100-102, 105-106, 155
embodiment, bodies 38, 43, 56-57, 75, 104-105, 160-161, 170
emotion 8, 55-56, 129, 133, 160-161
empire *see* colonialism, colonization
endurance *see* commitment
environmental education 24, 47-50, 76, 100, 119, 130, 164

erasure of history 6, 10, 38, 151
escape 4-5, 65, 127, 170
essence, essentializing (in research) 17, 23-24
Esteva, Gustavo 70, 85
ethnography 16-17, 26-27
evolution, evolving 156-157, 174

F

facilitation, facilitators 94-95, 110, 152
failure 11, 83, 122-123, 125, 134-135, 158-159, 174
Fairbanks, AK 89-91, 107
farming 35, 64, 69, 97-99
Faustian bargain 35-37, 42, 52
feminism 70-71, 126, 147, 156, 160
  feminist research 20-21
field notes 26
First Alaskan autonomy *see* Indigenous autonomy
First Alaskan education *see* Indigenous education
flourishing 10-11, 151, 162
food 64, 67, 69, 72, 76, 97, 123, 145
Four Immeasurables 129
freedom 43-44, 125, 151, 156
Friedel, Tracy 118-121, 151-152, 155, 163
friendship 46, 63, 73-75, 92, 133, 155
futurity 156-158

G

gardens 45, 73, 76, 98
gender 70-71, 122, 147, 153
generalizability (of research) 21, 23
generosity 78
genius 82-84, 86
Gandhi, Mahatma 72, 76, 135

global economy 65-66
goodness 9, 17-18, 23-24, 145
grading 7, 83, 153, 163
Greenwood cemetery 35-36, 51
Greenwood, David 28, 35-61, 147, 154, 158-160, 172
guilt 5, 10, 125
Gumbs, Alexis Pauline 156-157

H

Hampton, Eber 118
Happy Valley, PA 63, 71, 73-74, 87
Haraway, Donna 146, 150, 159
harm 10, 24, 124
harmony 9, 55, 57, 149
healing 129
hiking *see* being outside
history 5, 120, 156-158, 164
holistic fallacy (in research) 25
honesty 9, 55, 78
honor, honorable 9
hospitality, hosting 64-67
humility 71, 91, 96, 109, 135
hypocrisy 4-5, 12, 169-171

I

idealism 10, 127-128
Illich, Ivan 38, 70-74, 76-78, 81, 85
imagination 146-147, 170
impossibility 6, 10, 127, 145
Indigenous autonomy 90-92, 110-111, 114, 152
   Indigenous education 102-108, 118-121
   Indigenous epistemology 101, 121
   Indigenous knowledge 103, 105-106
   Indigenous research 90, 118-121

individualism 5, 10, 109, 144, 146, 149-151, 156-157, 165
industrialization 70, 98
inferiority complex 83, 86
inner self 9, 51-52, 55-58, 148
innocence politics 5, 10, 163
   see also purity politics
institutional education 38, 64-66, 105-106
institutional reform 139-140, 158
institutional violence 53, 84, 133, 154
interconnectedness 99, 120, 129
interdependence 129-130, 150-151, 159, 165-166
interpenetration *see* interdependence
interviews 21-22, 26-27
ivory tower 102-108

J

joy 79, 81-83, 85, 129-130, 133

K

Kahn, Richard 123-126, 152, 157, 160
Kamiak Butte 47-48, 50, 172
Kawagley, Oscar 95, 109-114
kindness 78, 84, 86, 129, 134-135
kinship 102, 119
Kodiak 112

L

Lakehead University 37, 48, 51
land-based economies 65, 97-98
land-based knowledge 100-102, 118-121, 126, 130-132

language 21, 37, 51, 92, 100-102, 104, 138-139
leadership 51, 126, 137
learning (integrity as learning) 156-161
   see also culturally relevant education
leverage of power 99, 121-123, 152-154, 164
liberation 125, 148, 162
lifestyle politics 5, 123
limitations (of research) 28-30
linguistic systems *see* language
listening 13, 21, 131-132, 152, 155, 169
living as learning 66, 69, 77, 139
localism 41, 64, 67, 72, 108, 139
love, loving 50, 60, 67, 73-74, 82, 86, 129-130
Luke, Howard 94-95, 110, 113

M

marginalization 70, 114
Martusewicz, Rebecca 132-135, 147, 152, 155, 157-158, 161
metaphor 22-23, 138
mindfulness 56-57
mistakes 11, 124, 159
Moore, Kathleen Dean 149
moral compass 108, 114, 135
moral dilemmas 77, 137
more-than-human communities 43-44, 69, 126-127, 131-133, 143, 155-156, 163, 166
   in research 22, 171-172
   multi-species collectivities 150
multi-layered resonance (in research) 23-24, 26, 28
mutuality 130, 151

N

Napoleon, Harold 110, 113
narrative analysis 22-23, 27-28
narrative inquiry 16-17, 21
narrative structure, form 27-28
natural world *see* more-than-human communities
neoliberalism 5, 36, 121-122, 143

O

Old Minto 93, 105-106
Oliver, Mary 171
Orr, David 72, 76
outdoor education 38-40, 49, 69, 77, 99-100, 102, 118-119, 163
outer self 52, 55-58, 169
overwhelm 54, 166

P

paddling *see* being outside
Palmer, Parker 9, 55, 85, 132
Palouse, Washington 35-37, 51
paradox 47-48, 53, 126-128, 139
paralysis 11, 145, 159
parenting 3-4, 98
participant observation (in research) 26
patience 134
Penn State *see* The Pennsylvania State University
photography (in research) 26
Piersol, Laura 130-132, 155, 163
place-based education 38, 40-41, 49, 100-102, 104-105, 118
place-based knowledge 21, 38, 46-47, 91
policymaking 111, 137
political strategy *see strategy*

portraiture 8, 15-32, 171-172
positionality 25, 91, 151-154, 171
possibility 11, 128, 145-147, 157, 166, 169-171
postsecondary education 6-8, 39, 51-54, 139, *see also* ivory tower
Prakash, Madhu Suri 63-87, 147, 151, 161
prefiguration, prefigurative politics 162-164
principles 134-135
privilege 10, 42, 57-58, 79, 121, 146, 152-154
process (as opposed to product) 157-158
productivity 40, 49, 58
purity politics 5-6, 10-11, 149

Q

queerness 148

R

racism 53, 119, 134-135, 144-145
    racial capitalism 5
reciprocity 19, 24, 119, 151, 161
reconciliation 76, 101
regeneration, regenerative 67, 81
reinhabitation 44-45, 48
relationality 11, 132, 152, 157
resistance 38-39, 44, 58, 148, 162-164, 170, 172
response-ability 11, 146-148, 150, 154-156
responsibility 42, 53, 128, 146, 154-156
    in research 18-19
rightness, right thing 54-55, 147, 170-171
root metaphors 138
Rural Education Caucus 92, 100-102

Russell, Connie 121, 152-153, 161, 165

S

Sartre, Jean Paul 127
scale 11, 144-149
scarcity (logic) 156, 170
Schindler's list 81
scholar activism 49, 121, 133, 139, 158, 165, 172
service
    academic service 74-75, 92
    serving(ness) 57, 114, 135-137
settler colonialism *see* colonialism, colonization
shame 124-125
shit 68, 75
Shotwell, Alexis 5-6, 10, 146-147, 149, 154, 170
Smith, Graham 111
social movement 48, 164, 172-173
social transformation 7, 53, 143, 145, 148-149, 162-166, 172-173
soil 67-69
solidarity 48, 151
sorrow 40, 78, 83, 160-161
soul 40, 42, 64
sphere of influence 153, 163
standardization (in education) 38, 73, 90, 101-103, 110, 120
standpoint *see* positionality
Starhawk 152
State College, PA *see* Happy Valley, PA
stay(ing) with the trouble 159-161
storytelling 8, 16, 20-24, 147
strategy 164-166, 173
strength 18, 139, 148, 174
struggle 42-43, 48, 53-54, 159-160
Stuchul, Dana 73-75, 82
subjectivity 17, 23, 46, 120

subsistence 66, 98-99, 106, 109
suffering 3, 6, 54, 79, 124, 130, 135, 154, 174
sustainability 48, 51, 69, 78, 125, 138-139

T

tenacity *see* commitment
tension 48, 54, 60, 159-160, 169
The Pennsylvania State University 63, 71, 73, 76, 87
thematic analysis (in research) 21, 27-28
Thoreau, Henry David 42-43, 49, 51, 60
Three Poisons 128-129
transformation of self 5, 51, 53, 72-73, 75, 123, 148
transformation of society *see* social transformation
trust 18-20, 29, 45-47, 69, 75, 83, 86
Truth and Reconciliation Commission of Canada 120
truth 13, 22-24, 27
    staying true 120, 133-135, 147-148, 157-158, 174
    truth value 24

U

UN Declaration on the Rights of Indigenous Peoples 110, 120

V

validity (in research) 19, 23-26

value alignment 11, 42, 53-54, 101, 132, 135-137, 144, 147, 158-160, 163, 170
veganism 123-126
verisimilitude (in research) 24-25
victimization 35-37
vigilance 131
virtue 13, 108, 143, 169
visioning 10-11, 45, 114, 157, 163-164, 170
vulnerability 8, 18-19

W

Walia, Harsha 162, 170
walking *see* being outside
Washington State University 37, 45-46
waste 68, 76, 149
weakness 18
white supremacy 4, 109, 120, 124, 133, 151
Whitman, Walt 39, 43, 53-54, 59, 158
wholeness 9, 28, 40, 43, 51, 56-58, 132, 137
Whyte, David 55, 59
wildness 43-44
Williams, Dilafruz 135-137, 152-153, 157, 165
workaholism 40, 122

Y

Yupiat 109-110

GENERAL EDITORS: CONSTANCE RUSSELL & JUSTIN DILLON

The [Re]hinking Environmental Education book series is a response to the international recognition that environmental issues have taken center stage in political and social discourse. Resolution and/or re-evaluation of the many contemporary environmental issues will require a thoughtful, informed, and well- educated citizenry. Quality environmental education does not come easily; it must be grounded in mindful practice and research excellence. This series reflects the highest quality of contemporary scholarship and, as such, is positioned at the leading edge not only of the field of environmental education, but of education generally. There are many approaches to environmental education research and delivery, each grounded in particular contexts and epistemological, ontological and axiological positions, and this series reflects that diversity.

For additional information about this series or for the submission of manuscripts, please contact:

> Constance Russell & Justin Dillon
> c/o Peter Lang Publishing, Inc.
> 29 Broadway, 18th floor
> New York, New York 10006

To order other books in this series, please contact our Customer Service Department:

> (800) 770- LANG (within the U.S.)
> (212) 647-7706 (outside the U.S.)
> (212) 647-7707 FAX

Or browse by series:

> WWW.PETERLANG.COM

www.ingramcontent.com/pod-product-compliance
Lightning Source LLC
Chambersburg PA
CBHW061715300426
44115CB00014B/2693